Casino Surveillance and Security: 150 Things You Should Know

Gary L. Powell
Louis A. Tyska, CPP
Lawrence J. Fennelly, CPO, CSS

ASIS INTERNATIONAL
Advancing Security Worldwide™

D1346786

Acknowledgments

We wish to thank Ann Longmore-Etheridge for giving us ideas that we used in Section C. A special thanks to Jim Goding, Derk Boss, and Douglas Florence.

We also wish to thank Al Bentley, Bob Del Rossi, James Stone, and Bill Zender.

In producing this volume, we are also grateful to our typist, Beth Boucher, and to Evangeline Pappas, our editor at ASIS International.

We wish to acknowledge with thanks Mark Ennis, who assiduously read the manuscript and made several suggestions that greatly improved the book.

Introduction

"A large part of our job is to observe for individuals who enter our property to steal from us or our guests."

From *Corporate Security Newsletter* 27
November 15, 2001

Have you ever tried to travel across the United States, Canada, or even Australia without directions, maps, or guides, and accompanied by a group of people? Well, that is what it is like working in a casino without directions or guidance. For many of us, Gary Powell and the books of Lou Tyska and Larry Fennelly have been our guides for years. Gary has been lecturing on casino security for over 20 years, and for the first time his notes from those lectures as well as additional materials have been put on paper.

I am grateful to these three individuals for spending countless hours over the course of a year to complete this work, which I believe will be around for a long, long time. I met with the authors, wrote, and reviewed various sections, and I firmly believe that casino loss prevention practitioners will benefit greatly from this text. I also believe that this book, for many years, will be a firm building block for those of us currently in the casino industry as well as those who will be entering into this specific arena of loss prevention.

Derk J. Boss, CPP, Chairman
ASIS Gaming and Wagering Protection Council

Table of Contents

Section A: Surveillance Room Operation

The Surveillance Department

The surveillance department is independent of the casino operations being monitored and usually reports directly to the general manager, vice president, or controller. Casino supervisory personnel normally work closely with surveillance and may request coverage of specific events or persons without having to go through the higher chain of command; they can go directly through the surveillance director. This also promotes good teamwork and good communication.

1.

Camouflaged Holes: Surveillance Room[1] — Part I

There is a phenomenon in dealing with personnel known as a *camouflaged hole*. This is where there is an appearance of someone being there when there really isn't. It occurs when it is thought someone is able to do a job, is being paid to be there and do the job, yet is not doing it and, in fact, cannot. This can be total, or it can be partial. For instance, if a surveillance investigator is thought to have extensive knowledge of gaming, yet is weak in a certain area, such as craps or roulette, and conceals the information from his seniors and other workers, there is a camouflaged hole. He can't handle a certain game, yet no one knows this.

It is much better for everyone involved if it is known that the person has a weak spot. Several things can be done to handle it. The person can be partnered with someone who really does know the game; the person can be coached and tutored to pick up the necessary knowledge and learn what is needed to know to watch the game. Since it is known to superiors that the person is weak on a game, it is not even too far out of line to get a pit manager into the surveillance room to review a section of tape on a questionable payoff.

But if the person's weak spot is concealed and nothing is done to handle it, he or she will end up reviewing a game and giving false information to executives or pit personnel to try to conceal a weak spot. This reduces the credibility and effectiveness of the surveillance department and in an extreme case could even put the casino at risk, if a false evaluation were acted upon.

---

[1]Permission to reproduce obtained from the author, Jim Goding.

2.

Camouflaged Holes: Surveillance Room[2] — Part II

It is also possible to have a complete hole camouflaged. This occurs when a person believes he or she has extensive education and knowledge in the field of gaming, yet is unable to evaluate performance on a game, spot crooked activity, or see outpoints or bad procedure being used to conceal theft or cheating. The person would feel that, because of all the courses he or she took, he or she was a competent investigator, yet would always be finding ways to get others to do the work of reviewing incidents, watching games, etc. One could become quite clever at concealing the lack of knowledge even from oneself.

Unfortunately, there is another use for a camouflaged hole. Hunters know it and combat personnel know it; it's a trap for the unwary. You are walking along confidently on the trail, and all of a sudden the ground disappears from under your feet; you fall ten feet onto sharpened stakes.

Or, more familiarly to most of us in these peaceful times, you take a lunch break, leaving the room in the care of your partner. He or she gets a craps, blackjack, or wheel review, or a question about a person's play from the shift manager, and is incompetent to handle it. Your partner gives an erroneous evaluation of a tape review. Guess who falls in a hole? You, your boss, and anyone else who has helped to camouflage the hole by covering for the person who is weak.

You would be better off having no personnel than to have someone whom you thought could do the job, but who, in fact, could not. At least then you can compensate for the hole. This also applies to personnel in other areas. Sometimes we find that a particular floor person is incompetent, or simply doesn't know the job: he or she lets dealers get away with poor procedures, finds other things to do besides supervise, etc. This, too, is a camouflaged hole, unless reported. Here we have a definite function. Through careful reporting of the problem, the person in question can be brought up to a level of competency or otherwise handled on their own chain of command, based on information (not opinion) passed to them from the surveillance department.

---

[2]Permission to reproduce obtained from the author, Jim Goding.

The cure for a camouflaged hole is to identify it and report it. Once known (the covering of branches and leaves has been removed), it is much more difficult to fall into the trap. Steps can be taken to fill it in or otherwise handle it.

If you have weak spots, be sure your partner and your supervisor know about them, so that they can be handled.

3.

Current Gaming Crimes[3]

Most, if not all, gaming properties have slot clubs and other reward programs for their players to develop a player base and to attract high action players. These clubs and programs usually return comps and even cash to deserving players. As most surveillance personnel know, where there are comps and cash to be had, someone will figure out a way to take it illegally.

It has been my experience that in every slot club and reward program, no matter how well designed or controlled, there is the possibility that someone, whether it is an employee or someone from outside, will circumvent the program's safeguards and illicitly obtain undeserved comps and cash. When this occurs and is finally detected, it is common that the theft was occurring for a substantial period of time and that it costs the property thousands of dollars. Unfortunately, all too often, the perpetrator is a trusted employee.

Here is a recent example of this type of theft. A surveillance agent for a Las Vegas casino was patrolling the pit areas and happened to place his camera onto a pit clerk who at that time appeared to be performing her normal duties (entering player information into the computer). However, as the agent continued his observation, he noticed that the clerk was calling up different accounts and writing the information from some of the accounts onto a piece of paper. The clerk then accessed on the computer the accounts she had identified and, while the agent watched, changed the accounts from the name of the player to that of her own.

Investigation determined that the clerk had identified, accessed, and changed into her own name dormant player accounts that had reward points available. Although she was a pit clerk, she was accessing slot accounts. Continued observation and investigation determined that the clerk on this one occasion obtained $137 in cash value that she redeemed for herself later that day.

The surveillance department, desiring to put together necessary evidence of the activity and to ascertain its extent, continued to monitor the clerk and the other clerks assigned to the pit.

Further investigation revealed that the clerk, an employee of one year, had begun illegally accessing player accounts shortly after she started working for the property. Not only did she take points from dormant slot accounts, but also

---

[3]Reproduced from Derk J. Boss, CPP, *SINdicate* 2 (January 2001). Permission obtained to reproduce.

established fraudulent table games accounts for her boyfriend and her roommate, entering enough false play to justify comps for free hotel stays and gourmet dinners.

Although the surveillance was able to verify that a total of $870 in comps and cash was stolen by the clerk and her associate during a two-week period, the total amount was unknown. However, it was certain to be much higher over the period of a year.

The clerk was arrested by Nevada Gaming Control based on the evidence provided by the surveillance department.

Prevention/Detection Techniques

- Observe employees who have access (especially those with account editing privileges) to sensitive information on a routine basis for suspicious or unusual activity.

- Ensure employees use computer logons and passwords to prevent unauthorized access. If left on and unattended, computers should be equipped with a screen saver requiring a password.

- Ensure that sensitive transactions such as changes to accounts and access into dormant accounts generate exception reports to the auditing department.

- Ensure that someone is responsible and held accountable for reviewing daily exception reports. In the case above, it was determined that exception information was readily available, and if followed up would have exposed the crime almost immediately.

4.

Funny Things Seen on Closed Circuit Television (CCTV)

1. One of the best we have seen was on a roulette wheel. The dealer cocked her hand for a good fast spin and released the ball. The ball flew out of the wheel and directly into the cleavage of a well endowed young lady sitting two spots from the wheel head. Truly a one-in-a-million spin. The lady cracked up and then reached in and retrieved the ball, holding it up for all to see.

2. We caught one on video that really was unique to Las Vegas. Standing at a crap table was Elvis from Hong Kong. He was about 6 feet tall and weighed 150 pounds. He had the Elvis wig, burnt-cork sideburns, sequined vest, wide-lapelled shirt, and his legs stuck out the bottom of his pants at least six inches above his shoes. But he was having a ball.

3. We saw a wealthy casino patron placing bets on a crap table with his left hand, while, in his right hand was an electric razor, which he was using to touch up the stubble on his shaven head.

4. One criminal got caught in a casino by sheer stupidity. After raking all available coins from behind the drop-box doors, and making his way to the exit, he actually turned around and returned to the bank he had raided and straightened the chairs. That's where he was when the security people reached him.

5. A dealer was observed moving a stack of one-hundred-dollar chips; the dealer clearly moved them into the waistband of his trousers. The shift manager was notified and the tape was reviewed. The dealer was asked to remove the chips, which he did before he was placed under arrest and handcuffed. The tape was used as evidence at his trial.

6. Front man for a small con artist was dressed up in an Elvis look-alike outfit; he sang a song and people put down their cups with money to applaud while his associate stole the cups. They fled and the cameras followed; security was advised of the direction they were headed. They were stopped, arrested, and handcuffed. Both claimed not to know each other, but the tape didn't miss a step.

7. A guy, bill in hand and reaching for the validator, passed out on the slant-top slot machine.

8. Brides in full wedding regalia, right down to the train and veil, playing craps and pulling handles on the slot machines.

5.

Internal Theft: The Players Club[4]

Each morning at the casino, a personnel department manager stopped by a vendor kiosk for a cup of coffee. She always purchased the same type and size of beverage and paid the same amount. One day, she noticed that although the clerk had charged her properly and had given her the correct change, the clerk entered the transaction into the register for a lower price than what the coffee sold for. The manager reported what she had seen to the surveillance department.

A video audit of the coffee kiosk was conducted within hours of the report. Careful observation determined that the clerk was using a variety of methods to steal company funds, including overringing, hitting the "no sale" button, and accepting payment for items in the form of "tips" placed directly into her toke jar. The clerk set the stolen cash aside inside the cash drawer for easy identification. At the end of her shift, she removed the cash and commingled it with her tips.

Investigators initiated an audit to include all hours of operation and all employees—not just the one who had raised suspicions. The audit revealed that all four kiosk operators were embezzling company funds by the same methods.

When confronted, the employees admitted to their theft. They were prosecuted and forced to make restitution based on the amounts each had admitted stealing, although they probably stole far more. A follow-up investigation revealed that the coffee kiosk had no written operational procedures, no internal controls, and no daily inventory report. Moreover, no supervisor was directly assigned to monitor the kiosk or its employees. Those bitter realizations were a jolt of reality.

---

[4]From Derk J. Boss, CPP, and Douglas L. Florence Sr., CPP, "The Sure Hand of Surveillance," *Security Management*, September, 2001. Alexandria, Virginia: ASIS International.

6.

Internal Theft: The Bartender Is Dishonest[5]

Staff crime is common in all casino retail point of sale (POS) environments, including bars and lounges, gift shops, ticket sales counters, and hotel registration.

For instance, to encourage guests to feed the slot machines, casinos normally provide free drinks for extended play. The bartender is usually trusted to dispense these complimentary drinks. A dishonest bartender can easily enter a comp transaction into the register when he or she makes a sale to a non-player who paid for a drink. The cash is then set aside for later retrieval by the bartender.

There is one classic tell for this kind of theft. To retrieve the correct amount from the till, thieving employees must keep a mental total of the overage they have accumulated. Many keep this tally symbolically by using items such as cocktail straws or pennies. When surveillance sees a cashier rubbernecking and then placing small objects into piles beneath the countertop, in a drawer, or in other places, investigators are notified.

In the audit, surveillance investigators compare videotape of the drinks served to the guests at the bar to the register transaction report. Many casinos are also installing integrated, real-time POS systems that show all the cash register details on a monitor in addition to video coverage.

---

[5]From Derk J. Boss, CPP, and Douglas L. Florence Sr., CPP, "The Sure Hand of Surveillance," *Security Management*, September, 2001. Alexandria, Virginia: ASIS International.

7.

Internal Theft: The Gift Shop[6]

The gift shop comes with its own set of typical schemes. At one casino, the accounting department requested an audit of the casino gift shop after it reported that, for unknown reasons, the cost of sales had increased significantly over the preceding few months. The investigators immediately established continuous CCTV monitoring of the gift shop, its employees, and its customers.

It soon became apparent that shoplifters were regularly hitting the store. Once the problem was detected steps were taken to catch the thieves. After a number of these apprehensions and arrests, word got out that the casino gift shop was no longer an easy target and shoplifting decreased. Yet the cost of sales failed to improve.

The investigators then began a video audit of each cashier. It showed that these employees were eating and drinking store items without paying for them, but these losses didn't completely account for the discrepancy.

As surveillance continued, one cashier became the focus of attention for regularly violating store policies and procedures. She did not always issue receipts to customers, she worked out of an open drawer, she failed to ring up some items, and she appeared to count her drawer four to five times during her shift.

Investigators obtained the register tapes for transactions handled by this cashier. The tapes were then compared with the videotape of the cashier's activities. It was determined that the cashier was embezzling company funds through several means. For example, she would frequently sell items such as soda, water, cigarettes, and phone cards but would not enter the items into the register. (The cashier was able to track the overages by printing out a balance report of her legitimate sale transactions.) Alternatively, she sometimes rang up only part of the purchase but charged the customer for the correct total.

At the gift shop, cashiers who had been relieved took their drawers to a storage room. No cameras were located in this area. The dishonest cashier used this room to remove the stolen money and place it in her purse. Investigators concluded that she was stealing an average of $70 per day. She had been employed at the casino for more than a year.

---

[6]From Derk J. Boss, CPP, and Douglas L. Florence Sr., CPP, "The Sure Hand of Surveillance," *Security Management*, September, 2001. Alexandria, Virginia: ASIS International.

When interviewed, the cashier admitted she had taken the money to pay for food, as she regularly gambled away her salary.

As a result of the surveillance, a "blind drop" system was initiated, in which cashiers take their banks directly to the cage for verification and deposit. A CCTV camera was also installed in the back room. When the surveillance department checked with accounting 30 days later, the cost of sales had returned to normal.

8.

Internal Workings of a Surveillance Room and the Responsibilities of Each Employee Down the Line

We will start first with the responsibilities of the surveillance director.

1. Have manpower: you have to have the proper number of staff.

2. Assign work schedules:

    a. There is a right shift for everyone; you will find that there are people who love to work the graveyard shift. We light candles for these people.

    b. Remember that when doing this for your room, you should state that no one is actually guaranteed certain days off or shifts, and that everyone should be flexible to cover any shift that is necessary for the convenience of the property.

    c. It is highly recommended that you include that the oncoming shift be there ten minutes before relieving the previous shift for the purpose of debriefing, so one shift does not leave with another one coming on without knowing what is going on down on the casino floor.

    d. Also included in your scheduling should be provisions if the incoming shift will be short-handed because of sickness or someone being late. The off-going shift will supply an operator to stay over four hours, and the new shift will then call an operator four hours early from the next shift to relieve the operator who stayed late.

3. Evaluate the employees' progress and performance.

4. Observe your employees, see where their skill level is and provide proper training in weak areas.

5. Coordinate activities of the people that work in your room.

    a. Gaming training

    b. Equipment training

    c. Supervisor training sessions (sexual harassment classes, supervisory classes, disciplinary handling, hiring and firing, etc.)

6. Accommodate all areas of training that your employees may seek, should it be related to their actual working progress.

7. The surveillance director must also interview prospective employees, hire people, and determine by written and/or verbal questions, or actual testing, any special skills of the applicant.

A manager should ensure high standards of performance by supervisor operators. These people must set an example for the investigators on their shift. The manager or supervisor must ensure adherence to corporate policies and regulations both inside and outside of the surveillance room. The surveillance manager is also, unfortunately, responsible for discipline, suspensions, and terminations of substandard, unsatisfactory, or insubordinate employees.

9.

Cooperation With Casino Management

Our next area of management within the surveillance room will be cooperation with the casino management.

Your surveillance director should have an excellent rapport and work as a team with casino management with the protection of the company assets and liabilities in mind. To do best for the company, you should have an open enough relationship with the casino management to enable you to recommend procedure improvements; report casino employees' evaluations as requested by casino management, such as dealer audits; and report casino employee infractions. We prefer the procedure violation report.

The surveillance director must also inform the casino management of suspicious activities when appropriate (unless you are watching casino management, of course). The surveillance director must notify his or her chain of command of actions taken in response to any type of cheating, theft, or embezzlement, or anything that may be a danger to the company's assets or liabilities.

The surveillance director must ensure cooperation with casino management requests such as special observations on dealers, hands per hour, wheel audits, and other similar things.

10.

Cooperation With Security

A important function of a surveillance room is cooperation with security. You must work as a team, surveillance as the eyes and the ears to observe and document; the security staff as the enforcement arm of the surveillance department. The surveillance director maintains a liaison and open lines of communication with the chief of security.

This can be a difficult function if both the surveillance director and the security director cannot leave their egos at home and remember what their assigned duties are. In this line of work, egos can cost the company money beyond estimate.

11.

The Daily Functions of a Surveillance Director

Special Investigations

To direct special surveillances requested by casino management, security management, or as required by specific department heads to help protect the properties assets and liabilities.

Surveillance rooms may conduct their own special observations. When a surveillance room is doing a special confidential observation, there is a good reason for it. You do not want to turn information over to casino management on someone only suspected of stealing, cheating, or working with conspiracy with other people. You want to have all your t's crossed and i's dotted before you turn information over on suspected suspicious activity, so as not to hang a curtain on that employee's head unjustifiably.

Your surveillance director must also review the results of special surveillances and act according to the evaluations conducted.

Again, it is important to maintain an open relationship with casino management on gaming infractions and violations and how to prevent future infractions. Your surveillance director must reach out and maintain a liaison with the local law enforcement and local and state gaming divisions.

A key responsibility of a surveillance director is to establish and maintain a casino employee information file with photo identification. This helps special investigations by providing identification of the employees without necessity of making a phone call and possibly damaging the integrity of your investigation.

The surveillance director must review and evaluate daily shift reports (DSR) and then take whatever action is necessary. It's a good idea for the surveillance director to spot-check and review videotapes, observing what the surveillance team has been observing on their working monitors. The working monitor tape is a history of the activity throughout the shift, as well as the documentation in the daily shift reports.

12.

Equipment

The surveillance director has to depend on the shift supervisor's advice on a daily basis as to what is going on with the equipment, because the manager cannot be there twenty-four hours a day. An equipment card or good repair log must be maintained for all CCTV repairs for documentation of the equipment status. It will ensure proper functioning of equipment to maintain these logs and keep dates and costs of maintenance performed by staff, and also outside maintenance purchases when necessary.

13.

Supervisors

The surveillance director must have dependable supervisors, also known as leads, on each shift. A supervisor's daily function is to oversee his or her shift and to report everything of note to the surveillance director.

It is highly recommended that you have your supervisors arrive in the surveillance room ten minutes before the shift change to obtain a debriefing from the prior shift, check equipment operation, look at any special assignment for operator duties, and check shift schedules to make sure that everyone is where he or she should be.

Supervisors should also recommend to the manager personnel for hiring, promotion, discipline, and termination.

The surveillance director should lean heavily on his or her supervisors to conduct on-the-job training on casino operations and equipment.

A supervisor is responsible for cooperating with casino management:

1.   Documenting procedure infractions.

2.   Conducting close watch surveillances requested by the manager or casino management.

3.   Initiating or continuing special surveillances directed by the director of surveillance.

4.   Informing the director of surveillance of special observation requests from other departments.

5.   Immediately notifying the director or manager of surveillance of any gaming violations.

Supervisors should always represent the director of surveillance in his or her absence and make the appropriate notifications. In other words, if the manager cannot be contacted and there is a serious issue on the casino floor, the supervisor must contact the next step up in the chain of command to make the proper notification. There is no reason not to brief the appropriate people just because one person on the team cannot be reached.

14.

Investigators

Key elements of the team are the surveillance operators—also known as investigators—the crew that sit at the helm and operate the cameras. They should always arrive a few minutes early for their shift and take a look around the surveillance room to see any "specials" that may be going on. They should check picture quality and make sure all equipment is running, and receive any pass-downs from the prior shifts in order to continue the operations.

It is a good idea for each shift to set out the tapes for the next shift's tape change and ensure that each tape is rewound completely. Playbacks should be checked on all recorders hooked up through a switcher, approximately ten to twenty minutes after tape change and this is noted in the Daily Shift Report (DSR).

All recording devices should be checked at least once every hour during the shift to ensure proper operation; noted in the DSR.

The surveillance operator receives any particular duty assignments for that shift from the supervisor. The operator makes appropriate entries in the DSR.

The operator must immediately notify the lead or the supervisor of that shift of any suspicious or unusual activities, no matter how odd it may sound.

It is up to the entire surveillance team to maintain cleanliness of room and equipment. Everyone should chip in to make the working environment healthy and comfortable.

The operators should receive periodic on-the-job training from the supervisors. The surveillance operator is responsible for maintaining familiarity with all local and state laws, corporate procedures, and hotel department regulations and publications. Surveillance operators who observe any unusual occurrences should immediately bring them to the attention of the supervisor, who will then make an appropriate determination of the severity of the issue. The supervisor will then initiate notification of appropriate personnel as appropriate.

Either the surveillance director or director of security should be responsible for reporting criminal violations to local law enforcement or gaming agencies, as appropriate. Other department heads—casino manager, slot manager, etc. — may also make these reports. Normally casino internal policies will determine who actually contacts law enforcement.

The operators maintain a chronological log in the DSR as well as any other reports generated of all events and who has been notified. The operator's sole job is to observe, record, document, and report.

15.

Documentation

The video documentation—the visual evidence, the face shots and the activities of all the suspects and witnesses—is so important. You are able to determine and log on tape as evidence table or slot house numbers, date and time, further documentation of continued incidents, and any other pertinent data videotape can acquire. There will be times when your surveillance personnel will observe activity that is obviously criminal, such as using optic devices in slot machines or monkey paws or physical things done on a game.

There will be other activity observed that, because of the persons involved or their actions, will just be suspect.

The primary function of the operator is to observe and document, to monitor, and to notify the appropriate chain of command, security, or the appropriate law enforcement agency, depending on your state, that has the responsibility for detaining the individuals or taking them into custody.

The surveillance operator, however, may be the person who initiates the actions and the investigation and makes observations that may very well establish that a crime is being committed.

The surveillance operator must at all times maintain the closest contact with his or her supervisor and security on these types of operations.

In other words, you are providing security the probable cause and the reason to believe that an individual or individuals has acted criminally on your property, which, dictates the right to detain the person.

A surveillance operator observing any potentially criminal activity should immediately institute the following steps.

1. Make sure a time-date stamp is synchronized on the respective monitors.

2. Get good coverage from at least three different angles, if possible.

3. Identify the table number or the slot bank number or other location on video.

4. Get clean coverage of suspects, dealers, and pit or other personnel.

5.   Log the tapes by number in the Daily Shift Report (DSR) and any other reports. (The original recording tapes may be called for by the judicial system to be used as evidence.)

In addition, the operator should attempt to log and record information such as age, race, sex, height, weight, description of clothing, and any other information that would help identify a suspect or associates. He or she should also take as many pictures as necessary to identify the suspects, associates, set-up personnel, and any activity in which the suspect may be involved.

All this information, as mentioned earlier, will be detailed and logged in your DSR, and an incident report will be written including time, date, and places. The operator should try to answer the who, what, where, when, and how questions in the report.

In all situations where a person or persons are suspected of committing a crime on your property, the Surveillance Director must be notified immediately, and will determine whether the local gaming authorities or local or state law enforcement agencies must be called.

A large part of the surveillance operator's job is to watch the employees and watch the money. The techniques by which a dishonest person will attempt to steal money shouldn't be underestimated. Any employee who has access to or is entrusted with assets of the property is in an excellent position to steal and/ or conspire and not get caught.

Sometimes employees who have never thought of stealing before may be tempted. Employees should know that the corporation will take aggressive action and counter-measures to discipline or prosecute dishonest employees.

Throughout the day the surveillance staff deals with other company employees in numerous departments. This communication has an effect on any relationship and teamwork with other departments. Surveillance personnel are generally recognized as essential elements in today's business to protect the company's assets and liabilities. An improper attitude or demeanor in communication with other departments can damage teamwork or any future cooperative relationship. While it's true that surveillance works with these various departments, surveillance does not work for them.

Always be courteous and efficient when dealing with other personnel. For example, phones should be answered, "Surveillance, this is Gary."

16.

Taped Evidence

The value of taped evidence in legal action is beyond estimate. Video has been used to obtain numerous solid convictions. The sight of the cameras alone has been a proven deterrent. Seeing cameras set for face shots at casino cage windows and counters usually makes one think twice before stepping up to that window to cash a fraudulent check.

If an incident out of the ordinary is detected by an operator, he or she immediately notifies the appropriate chain of command. During the early part of an operator's shift and throughout the shift as necessary, it is wise if the operator does a systematic review of all table games, slot areas, keno, hard count and soft count rooms, and the cage to make sure the coverage is pertinent to that shift's operation. This systematic review should also be logged on the Daily Shift Report (DSR). If something is later questioned in the DSR, all you have to do is pull the working monitor tape and see the record in its entirety.

17.

The Daily Shift Report (DSR)

We have been talking about the DSR, which each shift is required to maintain. Now let us go to the preparation and completion of a DSR. The DSR starts at the beginning of each shift.

The heading should be filled out, including the names of the persons working the shift, time shift starts and ends, and the date.

An equipment check should be done at the beginning of the shift and logged in the DSR. From this point on, throughout the shift, the equipment should be checked approximately once an hour; this is logged and noted in the DSR.

All entries written in the DSR should be readable and as complete and self-explanatory as possible.

An operator should even log late entries. If an operator was busy and forgot to make a particular log entry, enter it in later. You would write "late entry" and the time that you are putting in the late entry.

A DSR entry may simply refer, after time entry and a brief one-or two-line summary, to an Incident Report (IR) or Procedure Violation Report (PVR).

A PVR gives all details (what, who, when, where and how) of any violation of company policy, rules, procedures, or law. An IR is informational and gives all the details on any actual criminal activity by nonstaff or suspicious activity or any other incident that is not in violation of any company policy. These reports provide a permanent record on anything for which you could later desire information. It is the responsibility of the operator and the shift supervisor to maintain the DSR. Each listing in the DSR should include the name and the position of the person calling, a brief description of the incident or actions taken by surveillance, and any response to the call.

Although it is well known that the surveillance department does not actually work for casino personnel, every effort should be made to comply with casino personnel's requests for assistance. All information should be kept in the strictest confidence, and surveillance personnel must not make smart cracks, at cost of their jobs.

All outside contacts that we must remain cooperative with are valuable sources of information necessary to run a surveillance department. It's amazing how you can track a particular incident through several different departments.

At the beginning of each shift and after you start your DSR, you should read all prior DSRs written since the last time you were on duty. It's a good idea to make it mandatory for all operators and all other surveillance personnel to initial the DSRs, confirming that their contents are understood. If any entries are not understood or instructions are not clear the operator should ask about them immediately.

Surveillance personnel must always exercise good judgment in how they relay important or sensitive information. Always get the opinion of your fellow team members, because an error of judgment could be very embarrassing to your department as well as very expensive for your property if a court case results. The key to any successful surveillance department is that they all work together as a team, not as individuals and not as a shift. In other words, if an investigation is being done by the day shift and the area of concern is still present in the casino, the oncoming swing shift must continue with the investigation so as not to ruin it by failing to acquire and document vital information.

If there should be an internal problem in the department, you should discuss it with the supervisor immediately. If the operator is not satisfied, then he or she should request to see the director.

Overall, the primary function of the surveillance department is to protect the property's assets and liabilities. This is accomplished by providing a confident and well trained crew, as well as a surveillance room with equipment that operates and functions properly. Surveillance personnel should be able to detect and prevent persons or groups of persons from cheating or stealing internally or externally.

Most important—we cannot stress this enough—is that you always put the protection of your guests and the visitors to your property first. Not putting the welfare of your guests first could cost your corporation billions of dollars. So surveillance rooms, through proper documentation, recordings, and written reports, assist in protecting our guests and employees.

18.

24-7

Most surveillance departments are a 24–7 operation, meaning twenty-four hours a day, seven days a week. This assures that every credit, every marker, every fill, every transaction is covered on video to ensure proper handling procedures and protect against embezzlement and theft. There are times when floor surveillance may be necessary to get a particular angle that you could not see with available cameras on a table game, slot machine or slot machine bank. You should not be overdressed or underdressed for the environment of the casino floor.

You become familiar with the people on the casino floor. Whatever type of surveillance operation you are conducting, you get to know these people; you get to know them by name, by sight. It is important to realize that even though you know who these people are, regardless of their position within the company or their reputation, every person is subject to the temptation of stealing money. When large sums of money are present one must cross all t's and dot all i's and exercise caution and discretion regarding what information is detailed in reports or video recordings. The surveillance operator must always have in mind the internal security of the surveillance department.

The presence of large amounts of cash and negotiable items attracts an undesirable element, as well as tempting the most trusted employee. The surveillance department is an essential and vital link in the chain of procedures designed to protect the casino's assets. This includes protecting the honest players as well.

Surveillance has many functions: not only detecting violations of procedure, laws, and local state regulations, but providing, by the presence of its cameras, deterrents against violations. We have also mentioned the value of the video in prosecuting criminal activities.

Everything must funnel through the proper chain of command. This will ensure the full integrity of your surveillance room. Security should notify the surveillance department of suspected persons or unusual activities noted or observed. This type of communication is a vital tool for achieving the end result of protecting the casino's assets and interests.

19.

Development of Your Case: Taping and Maintaining Records of Illegal Activity

The following fifteen points are what is needed to build a case:

1.   Tapes must clearly show the full sequence of what has occurred.

2.   It is of vital importance to know the layout of your casino floor and all the possible camera angles available. Questionable acts must be seen and recorded clearly.

3.   Keep in mind that if you show a videotape in court, you will not be showing it to other gaming professionals. The jury may be made up of individuals not familiar with viewing videotape to ascertain illegal actions.

4.   The tape must clearly show who has committed the action or crime. Make sure you get a clear face shot of the individual in question.

5.   At a particular area, table game, or slot machine make sure you get the number of the game on video and associate the person or incident with that area. Always try to keep a part of the individual somewhere in your field of view while getting these identifying characteristics. On a game, make sure that you identify the dealer. You may be watching a customer for a possible past-posting on your roulette wheel, and as time goes on you see that the dealer is actually on a conspiracy.

6.   The tape must clearly show when the incident occurred. As mentioned earlier, with a time-and-date generator it is very easy to document the time of the incident. This is why you always make sure that the equipment is in good working condition and why you check it on an hourly basis.

7.   Trust us—take it from experience—it is not fun bringing a tape to court that tears or the quality is so poor nobody can make out what is on the tape. The defense loves that. Of all headaches we have had, the worst is a tape of an incident that occurred on March 4, 1991, and the tape read January 1, 2001. This could be very embarrassing and costly to the company.

8. The tape should clearly show where the incident occurred—again, identifying the surroundings. If the incident is happening at a table game or slot machine, make sure that you document the table number, the machine or bank number, and the people around the area.

9. Once you get all of this on tape, you must maintain the tape for the continuity of evidence.

10. You must have a safe area under lock and key for your evidence, located in a secure area so there is no doubt in the jury's mind that the evidence could not have been tampered with.

11. Make two copies of the criminal-activity recording immediately; this needs to be done because at some point a legal authority will want to take custody of your original evidence tape. If the original is not taken immediately by the arresting agency or responding agency, place it in an evidence bag, seal it, and fill out all the pertinent information on the outside of the evidence bag: tape number, date of incident, and a list of recordings and what they depict.

12. Dubs should be made of all original tapes for anyone needing to review the incident so that you don't need to keep signing the tapes out of the evidence lockup—the fewer hands that touch it the better. Dub tapes should also be made for your company's records.

13. Of course, your second copy should be placed in the files and saved as long as your company legal counsel feels it is necessary.

14. Place the original tapes and one of the duplicates in the evidence locker. The original should never leave the locker until it is given to the appropriate law enforcement agency or taken by the courts.

15. When a number of different tapes are involved, you will need to maintain logs of any tape or dub entered or removed from the safe and secured area or, for that matter, the surveillance room. Even if it was removed just for viewing it should be appropriately logged. There should also be a separate log of any tape that is released to an outside agency.

An example of this process: You suspect that you have a past-poster on a twenty-one game. You have plenty of tape, the VCR is recording, your time, date, and stamps are all correct. You get a good face shot of the player in question. Next you pan the table and get face shots of all the players, the dealer, and the table number. You angle back to the player in question, panning down to the table, trying to keep some part of him within the view. When the incident occurs, you have when it happened, where it happened, who committed it, and who else was on the game. You now take your tape, make duplicates, and log them and lock them into your evidence locker, carefully maintaining the chain of evidence. When all this is done you can sit back and smile, thinking of how bad that defense attorney will sweat when he reviews this process. It is a hard avenue for a defense to take when all those steps are followed.

20.

Evidence. What Does It Mean?

Let us define *evidence*.

> Evidence is the path by which disputed facts are proved to be true or untrue in any trial before a court of law or any agency that functions within the court system.

Its effectiveness is generally determined by how persuasive the evidence is to a jury. It is something that signals the existence or occurrence of something else. It could be the facts and circumstances that lead one to logically come to a conclusion that a crime has been committed.

21.

Burden of Proof

We must meet something called the *burden of proof* by producing the evidence and by convincing a jury or judge of its truth. There are two types of requirements that we know of for burden of proof: (1) to prove beyond a reasonable doubt that an incident occurred and (2) to prove that the person or persons did, in fact, commit the act.

Once we have our evidence, we have to get the evidence into court. This is called admissibility of evidence. The rules of admissibility determine which items of evidence the judge or jury may be permitted to hear, see, or read. It must be relevant evidence directly related to the crime in question. Evidence is relevant when it leads one, in reason, to prove or disprove any disputed fact.

22.

Hearsay

Hearsay evidence is simply evidence consisting of statements or other information received by a court from someone who is not present to testify under oath at a trial. They are not there to speak for themselves. It could be a written or typed voluntary statement, or a statement made verbally in the past. But the person is not there to be subject to any cross-examination by the plaintiff or the defendants. The value of hearsay evidence can be and will be questioned by the defense.

23.

Witnesses

One of the best pieces of evidence other than video documentation is a witness. Nearly all persons with knowledge that is relevant to the case can testify in the court of law. Witnesses are asked to stick with the facts rather than their opinions.

There is also a special category of witness: an expert witness, someone who is an expert in the field about which questions are being asked, or someone whose knowledge would help to prove a scientific fact or support a hard piece of evidence in the case. Such people would include doctors, fingerprint experts, accident reconstructionists, or a surveillance director or operator.

24.

Surveillance Department and Law Enforcement

Law enforcement uses surveillance in the gathering of the evidence. Law enforcement and security networks have developed a working understanding of surveillance departments and their capabilities. When a surveillance department is properly used, it can aid any law enforcement agency to develop its case, investigate it, and gain a conviction.

Video documentation is instant evidence for law enforcement use. Any crime that is viewed by surveillance will provide the arresting officer or agent with the ultimate unimpeachable eyewitness—videotape. Surveillance operations give law enforcement the ability to trace back a crime or incident over hours or even days. This is useful in trying to determine premeditation or conspiracy of a particular crime. Another important aspect of the work of surveillance in these times of litigation is that it gives the arresting officer a video backup against any charges of wrongdoing. When you detain people, if you are falsely accused of assault or battery on someone being detained, the video that you maintain in evidence could show otherwise. With proper coordination with surveillance, an arresting officer or agent will have video documentation of his or her arrest procedures, protecting him or her from any charge of abuse, such as when the security department detained an individual in the detention area.

The clandestine nature of a well maintained closed circuit television (CCTV) of a surveillance department enables total observation of an area without leaving the room giving the officer zero exposure. Surveillance room videotape procedures and tape library procedures give an officer knowledge that certain things and areas are always taped and held and maintains discretion as well, limiting the need-to-know basis of the investigation.

The CCTV room allows an officer to follow a subject and document the actions, times, and movements of the subject with greater visual accuracy because of the ability to switch cameras, as well as the ability to zoom in and out with the camera lenses rather than having to follow the subject, on foot through a crowd. This allows better and more accurate documentation of the detail of the crime and the individual being surveilled.

25.

The Gathering of Evidence: Cards

There are certain methods and precautions that must be used in the gathering of evidence, especially in casino-related crimes

Let's start with the cards used at a blackjack table, a baccarat table, or wherever cards are used. You suspect that there may be some type of marking or a daub (a foreign substance put on the back of a card in order to determine its value when face down) being used on the cards.

When gathering evidence from cards, handle the cards carefully by the edges and do not forcibly cause any rubbing or friction between the cards. You will find that there will be different groups of cards throughout the table. In other words, there are cards in the discard tray; cards in the shoe, both in front of and behind the cut card; cards on the table; and the player's and dealer's cards. It is very important to keep these groups of cards together with rubber bands, being careful not to rub or touch any suspected areas. Keep them all separate, and mark them separately as to their location on the table. Once you have done this, you place the cards into a paper evidence bag—paper being very important—so that no condensation can develop inside the bag. Condensation could possibly dissipate any markings that had been placed on the card or cause them to deteriorate overtime.

Make sure the cards that you seize are kept in the exact same order. This includes the cards in the shoe; sometimes it is just as easy to take the entire shoe, bag it and then bag the cards separately later. Just make sure that the cards will not fall out of the shoe while inside the evidence bag.

Cards at the position of a suspected cheat or coconspirator should be bagged separately and labeled as individual pieces of evidence taken from the suspect's possession. (First bag: "Cards and Daub substances taken from suspect's right front pants pocket." Second bag: "Daub substance found in suspect's left inside sport jacket pocket.")

Evidence from a gaming environment should be treated the same as any other type of criminal evidence. Protect the evidence and follow the same procedures to protect and document the chain of custody of it.

26.

The Gathering of Evidence: Slugs

Slugs are fake tokens, typically made of lead, intended to duplicate whatever denomination of coin or type of house tokens used in a slot machine.

In gathering evidence where slugs have been used, first check the payout tray of the slot machine(s). If there are any slugs in the payout tray, count and bag them separately. Check the coin accepter for a slug that might have stuck, which is common, and bag it separately. Open the machine and see if there are any slugs lying on top of the other tokens on the hopper; count and bag them separately. Bagging the ones on top of the hopper separately shows that these were the last coins played. This, along with video showing the last person to play the machine, is a nice little package for a jury.

Then go through the hopper and see what other slugs may match those found on the person or that had been played by the suspect. Bag those separately.

Check to see if the diverter has been reactivated in the open position. (The diverter is a device on the slot machine that alters the coin's path from the hopper into the drop box area.) Check the drop-box area for any slugs and follow the same procedure as the hopper: count and bag separately those on top and those mixed in with the other coins.

Do your homework while you are standing at the machine; get all the particulars. Write down the make of the machine, model number, serial number, bank number and house number. Example: GLP, upright, model # xxxx, Serial # xxxxx, $1, three-coin, three-reel, center pay-line, house #6130, bank 425."

At this point, with all the evidence bagged and documented separately, you will be able to link slugs in the drop area to slugs in the hopper and to slugs on the suspect's person, and possibly a match to where the slugs were manufactured.

27.

The Gathering of Evidence: Dice

If you feel you need to seize dice as evidence, we highly suggest you do your homework first. Observe the entire table first, taping everything if the opportunity exists. Establish a probable cause, reason to believe that dice have been altered or switched. Pay particular attention to the dice cup housing the idle dice as well as the active dice.

We have found it more efficient to stop the game and seize the dice between "points" while the stickman has control of them. This way you are able to keep all dice in your control rather than having to scramble for them. By this time most wagers have also been squared.

It is recommended that you never do a dice pickup for evidence without a partner. Always have a witness. Bag the active dice and inactive dice separately. Of course, attempt to have the best surveillance coverage available and ensure that when you seize the dice, the entire sequence of actions is clearly on tape.

28.

Techniques

Next we are going to get into techniques for the surveillance operator and law enforcement to use in investigating gaming crimes. There are investigative tools at your fingertips within the casino that you are responding to or where you work. Law enforcement uses the techniques of surveillance, a search of records or documents, the collection and preservation of evidence, and interviews.

An interview is a major part of any investigation. Remember that an interview is the complete opposite of an interrogation. The purpose of an interview is to identify parties pertinent to your investigation and gather documentation and evidence. The purpose of an interrogation is to question formally, a confession being the ultimate goal.

It always seems to pay off if the interviewer does some homework before conducting any interview. You want as much preparation as possible—as they say in the casino business, the edge. This is why we recommend you use surveillance as the first action if the situation allows. This enables you to get pertinent data you can use to form questions for your interview.

Collection and preservation of evidence is also recommended before your inter- views, if the situation allows. This must be a team effort with surveillance and the security department. You should be a good listener. Observe physiological factors as well as physical gestures and expressions of the person being ques- tioned. The biggest indicator of all is a break in the pattern, such as a physical motor skill. Surveillance cannot utilize sound, so they must know the proce- dures to be followed by all departments.

Here is an example: the act of dealing, to the dealer, becomes a "no-brainer." When a dealer has to break the regimented motor skill that he or she has learned, he or she must give thought to performing altered actions, and this breaks the pattern of the procedure. This is usually an indicator that something is wrong. It is usually a hesitation or fumbling of the cards or chips. Even if the move were perfected, a break in the pattern would occur. This is an indicator to the surveillance operator that something is wrong.

A surveillance operator primarily looks at a table as a fine, slow moving wheel. When the wheel pauses, as if stuck, then something had to have been altered, such as a change in the amount of wagers place by patrons who could be press- ing or pinching their bets. This is a strong indication that players are privy to information—they have some form of edge—not available to other players.

There are other indicators, known as "tells." Our bodies give off signals as to the comfort level they have with the actions being performed. This is similar to how a polygraph works. We need to train our own bodies to read and react to these tells so that we can focus our attention on the possibility of a problem.

For example, four individuals walk into your casino or your building; it's 105 degrees out, in the middle of the day, and they are wearing overcoats and ski masks. This should set something off, indicate to you that something is wrong.

29.

Rubbernecking

Another indicator is called rubbernecking: someone looks as if they are always wanting to know what is going on around them, rather than paying attention to what they are doing. Most patrons in the casino have their attention fixed on their own gaming or activities.

The fascination of gaming is not the winning of money, but the high of the excitement of the actual gambling act itself. To have money wagered and watch the wheel spin or the dice roll with your fate on the line is the draw. If someone is playing a machine without interest, and only seems interested in the person next to them, something is wrong. The body's stress level has a direct impact on functioning of the task at hand. If you notice the dealer's chip handling ability slowly become irregular, you could have a problem. An employee who constantly shortcuts procedures could be a problem waiting to happen. Are they constantly going to their body for a reason? Is the change person just bored and playing with the roll of coins or is he shortchanging the roll? A dealer leaning into or across a game in an uncomfortable position, or a dealer or cashier holding one hand in a cupped or other uncomfortable position are just a few of the tells that we would look for while working in a surveillance room.

30.

Indicators of Criminal Activity

Observing what is going on, without sound, can be beneficial to a law enforcement agent or a surveillance operator. There are certain indicators for each type of crime. For example, a pickpocket profile allows the surveillance agent to recognize a possible pickpocket working a crowd. Keep in mind that you can see this going on with just surveillance cameras and a monitor.

You may be watching a crowd of people entering a hallway and you notice individuals entering behind the crowd and backing out as the doors close. You can see individuals examining others' purses or going through wallets in an unfamiliar manner, individuals loitering around escalators or stairways and using them several times within a short period of time. You may see individuals talking together, then splitting up, only to converge and converse again in another location. An individual or individuals repeatedly asking people for change may be just a ruse to locate a target's money location or find out how much money they have on them. You may observe individuals carrying coats, scarves, sweaters, garments, bags, and so on, over their arms, or large shopping bags with handles that appear to be empty, so that it would be very easy to slip in a purse or other stolen merchandise from a store or casino. Individuals who seem to be paying a lot of attention to the people around them may be up to no good.

31.

Gamblers

What we are going to go into now is mostly related to casino games and game protection. We are going to start with the some basic information, breaking down what exactly gambling is and the different types of gamblers.

Gambling:

1. To play a game for money or property.

2. To bet on an uncertain outcome.

3. To bet something on a contingency—to take a chance.

4. To risk something by gambling, such as a wager.

5. To engage in an act having an element of risk.

6. To play a game of chance for stakes.

A key factor in these definitions is to bet on an uncertain outcome. This means betting without prior knowledge of what the results will be. If a person has knowledge of what the outcome will be, that individual is most likely involved in some sort of cheating, either alone or with a team of two or more, also known as a conspiracy. Cheating is a way of getting something by dishonesty or by deception. Our goal here is to strengthen our abilities to detect dishonesty and deception. We gain this knowledge by sharing information and pulling together resources both old and new.

There seem to be different types of gamblers, and we will attempt to break them down by category:

1. The *occasional gambler*: This constitutes the majority of today's gamblers. It is this type of gambler who helps make the casino business what it is.

2. The *degenerate* or *habitual gambler*: This person plays all the time, loses all his money, and cannot understand why the odds cannot be beat. This type of gambler craves to always be in action. Denomination is secondary. When this gambler wins, all the money is lost back, and then some. This is also the type of gambler who goes deep into debt to a loan shark.

3. The *skilled gambler*: This is a person who understands gambling more than the occasional or the habitual gambler. The skilled gambler will usually specialize in a particular area, such as blackjack. This is also the type of gambler who will cash in on the habitual gambler many times over in such types of games as poker or in noncasino gambling.

4. The *professional gambler*: The entity that owns and operates the casino. The casino business is like any other business having to do with money, such as a bank. The professional gambler is the middleman who risks his money against the player's wager. Also, a professional gambler is one who charges a commission, or *vigorish*, for his or her services.

5. The *system gambler*: The system gambler only exists in the mind of someone who honestly believes he has some type of system that can beat the odds or the "edge" of the house.

6. The *cheat*: This person makes money by cheating other players, different gaming devices, and, of course, the professional gamblers as well. A cheat can relieve you of your job.

32.

On Writing Reports[7]

Occasionally a surveillance crew feels that writing reports on personnel is of no value or is unjust to the people being reported on. After all, "There are many who are doing the same thing that are 'getting away with it,'" right?

Often these same surveillance personnel spend their time complaining about how poor the dealers are, how badly they interact with their customers, how easy it would be for change personnel to be stealing, how rich they could get if they worked in soft count or hard count, etc.

They complain about how the dealers don't spread cards, don't cut out cheques properly, have their hands in the trays, don't clear their hands, deal craps one-handed, toss cheques to the players, turn away from the tables, and do all the myriad little things that people who are not watched get away with. The common refrain is, "Things really weren't this sloppy when I was in the pit."

It is true that a good part of the responsibility for slovenly dealing and customer relations belongs with the actual supervisory personnel, from the dual-rate, part-time floor person right up to the casino manager. Middle and upper managers, especially, are often working in a vacuum of information. The lowest level of supervisors, such as pit floor people and slot floor supervisors, have many duties in addition to watching the dealers, change people, slot floor people, etc. They have paperwork without end, money tracking, fills, player cards, table cards, markers, comps and so on. And remember, it is often much easier and more personally rewarding to spend one's time talking with the players and doing the paperwork than trying to watch, isolate errors, and correct and train dealers (who usually feel they know more than the floor person), especially if one is only a single step up from dealing. In many casinos, lower-level supervisors have no authority to correct dealers or anyone else, and they often feel that reporting minor transgressions to the pit managers makes them sound as if they are whining.

There is a lot of pressure in some companies for the pit personnel, especially, to be watching the money, tracking the plays, watching for possible counters, rather than watching the personnel in their area for sloppy procedure and correcting it. Back-flash from juniors and a general lack of real authority over them plays a big part, together with a general lack of knowledge and training on how to handle recalcitrant juniors.

---

[7]Permission to reproduce obtained from the author, Jim Goding.

Thus, personnel start to get away with small things—poor card spread, inattention, tossing cheques, mixing tokes with the bank in the change booth. Pretty soon they feel they can get away with bigger things—going to the body without clearing hands, hustling the players, occasionally correcting their own errors, and so on.

After a while, the front line personnel know for a fact they aren't being watched and can get away with almost anything. A few of them—as much as ten percent—take the final step and begin stealing.

So you can see that the last line of defense for a casino corporation is in the Surveillance Room. You can also see that letting a dealer or change person get away with little things is really no favor to him or her. If they know they are being watched, they won't get as sloppy. You know, or even remember, that if the box person on a crap game is correcting his or her dealers regularly for the little things that lazy crap dealers do, they don't do them—at least with that boxman on the table.

If no reports are written from surveillance, then the upper levels of management—pit supervisors, shift managers, and casino managers—are operating in a vacuum of information. They don't know, except from personal observation, when the front lines are fluffing off. Trusting their own junior supervisors, they may think everything is just fine. It is, after all, not the job of a shift manager to watch dealers. His or her job is to coordinate and supervise pit supervisors, and through them, floor people and so on.

It is very possible for a dealer or change person, by not having been caught at little errors and lazy tricks, to get the idea he can get away with just about anything. It is also very possible for one, having been caught and corrected, to straighten up and fly right. We have seen it happen.

As long as lower-level personnel think they aren't supervised, they will get lazier and sloppier, and eventually a few of them will start taking what they can get. They'll get away with it, too, and even move up to supervisory positions. Then you have to detect their theft through the paperwork, a much harder job.

So you see, surveillance itself shares heavily in the responsibility for sloppy dealing and other bad habits. With no reports going out, no one feels they are being watched. So what is to stop them from getting lazier, sloppier, and even taking that first step into criminal activity?

So don't back off on writing reports. You might think that because everyone is getting away with it, it's unfair to single this one out. But that is because of poor supervision and a lack of reports in the past. Remember, every report also has on it the supervisor's name. He or she needs correction too. If you keep on writing those reports, the management has to eventually take note that things are getting really sloppy. One or two reports might get passed off, but fifteen or twenty will get attention. This is the process.

No one gets in really serious trouble from a single report, unless the error is grave and obviously intentional. However, unreported errors, building up over time, will, by reason of being ignored, be the downfall of many a dealer, floor person, cashier, change person, or other personnel.

Properly used, reports from surveillance can be very specific in pointing out areas or personnel that need further training. Rather than a heavy-handed, read-and-punish attitude, a manager can use surveillance reports to fine-tune his or her own organization from the supervisor level down.

Sooner or later things will get corrected. Some of those reports, and the correction that may have followed, might just give someone the idea he or she is being watched, and might prevent that first little theft.

33.

Put It in Writing[8]

If it isn't in writing, it doesn't exist; there is no record and the process failed. Reports should always be in writing. A written report, forwarded through proper channels, gets looked at, questioned, and clarified before reaching its final destination. Missing data can be filled in, errors in wording or attitude can be corrected, unclear information can be completed.

Writing also includes other permanent forms of data recording, such as videotape. In a surveillance room, a written report is nearly worthless without videotape backup. All reports are based on video evidence, and the raw data (tape) is always forwarded with the report or at least available on request by the correct person.

---

[8]Permission to reproduce obtained from the author, Jim Goding.

34.

Complaints, Ideas, and Suggestions

It is very common for the people actually doing the work, from the bottom levels to the top, to realize that the way something is being done is not the best way. It is even commonplace for people to have valid ideas as to better ways to do things. What is not, unfortunately, common is for someone to put a valid suggestion in writing and send it through correct lines to someone with the authority to make a change. The normal human way is to complain verbally about how bad something is. Someone might even suggest a good improvement, but unless it's in writing it will be ignored.

What is not realized is that a shift supervisor is not likely to remember the details of a suggestion because there are many other demands on his or her attention, most of them more *immediately* important. So those verbal suggestions are forgotten or are not correctly understood.

So if you have a good idea, the best way to get it implemented, or at least find out why it will not be implemented, is to write it down in detail and submit it to the executive in charge through your supervisor. This is also the only way you will ever get credit for the idea, if you are interested.

35.

Exceptions

In a surveillance room, certain types of reports are made verbally; however, they are always backed up by a written report, even if it's only an entry in the daily log. An example is the response to a request for a count on a certain player. An immediate phone report is made to the requesting pit manager or the casino shift manager, and an entry is made in the log. If a person is positively determined to be a card counter, a verbal report by phone is first made to the casino shift manager and then to the director of surveillance, and a written, detailed Incident Report (IR), which includes tape numbers and time, backs up the verbal report. Negative reports on card counters are made verbally by phone and an entry is made in the Daily Shift Report (DSR).

The idea is that, unless there is something in writing, everything is questionable, open to interpretation and error. In some cases, this can endanger your job or even the casino itself. Put it in writing.

36.

Chain of Command[9]

A chain of command is the series of positions in an organization through which reports and orders or requests for action are correctly routed. An example:

1.   Report originator: surveillance investigator.

2.   Surveillance supervisor.

3.   Surveillance director.

4.   Controller.

5.   General manager.

6.   (Then downward to) casino manager or slots director, security director, etc.

7.   Casino shift manager, etc.

There are two types of chains of command with which we are concerned in the surveillance room: the chain inside surveillance and all chains of command in other departments.

Within the room, our concern with chain of command is very simple. First, no one outside our own chain of command passes order to the surveillance room. This does not mean that we do not cooperate fully with other departments, handle requests, etc., only that orders into the room must be passed through our own chain of command. It also means that certain things are simply not done without approval of the surveillance director. Original tapes are not released to anyone, including enforcement agencies, without approval of the director, or in the case where he or she cannot be reached, a surveillance supervisor. Dub tapes are not made and released without at least informing the director. Special observations require the approval of the director, as does release of any information about the surveillance room, as well. Any information in writing goes out via the director.

---

[9]Permission to reproduce obtained from the author, Jim Goding.

That means that any order or request into the surveillance room to release information recorded in the surveillance room must pass through the director. Supervisors have the authority to handle releases only when the director cannot be reached, and only then in situations of urgency, such as arrests, when originals must be released to law enforcement agencies.

Internal matters having to do with surveillance personnel must pass through your chain of command. Complaints, bright ideas, suggestions, and requests for changes in personnel situations (such as schedules, shifts, vacations) pass through the supervisors to the director. Ideally, if an investigator wants the director to see a suggestion, he or she should write it down and give it to his or her shift supervisor, who will then pass it on to the director, unless it is completely off company policy. The investigator may want to go over such a suggestion with the originator, perhaps refining it or making it more viable. He may want to incorporate it into a larger package, or use it to back up something that is already being worked out.

Unfortunately, verbal suggestions most often get forgotten, and are seldom taken seriously. If you have a good idea, a suggestion for improvement of your department, the best way to get it to the attention of the people who can act on it is to submit it in writing through the chain of command.

Supervisors should be careful to attribute suggestions to the originator. Taking credit for a suggestion made by another is unfair and is, in fact, a bit of a betrayal. Such an action undermines the supervisor's position with his or her juniors, and when it is later found out about by seniors, it reduces the supervisor's credibility.

37.

Outside Chains of Command

Outside areas have their own chains of command as well, and it is vital to the proper functioning of our department and others that these be respected. Just as the surveillance investigator does not accept orders from outside the department, it is necessary that our own flow of information be directed to the proper terminals.

Surveillance verbal requests for immediate correction of a problem in the pit is a good example. A wheel dealer isn't waving off bets before the ball drops. This is a serious problem that has potential of costing the casino a lot of money. A report of a situation like this must go to someone who actually has authority to act to correct it and possibly (on their own authority, not ours) to do a "personnel correction," involving training or disciplinary action to the dealer. Immediate correction of the problem would fall to the casino shift manager. However, a report of the situation would travel through lines (up through the controller and general manager, down to the casino manager to the shift manager). Several such reports would point up a real situation requiring more major training or correction.

The investigator would report the problem to his or her supervisor, who would then contact at least a pit supervisor (not a floor person) and probably the casino shift manager. A report would be made to the director of surveillance; minimum report would be an explanatory entry in the Daily Shift Report (DSR).

More serious situations that could involve criminal prosecution or termination—such as detection of a dealer going south with checks or cash—would be reported, first and immediately, by the surveillance supervisor to our own director, as it involves gathering of evidence for a possible prosecution. The director, once evidence was gathered, would then report through command channels (controller, general manager, director of security, outside enforcement agency).

Such a situation carries with it major liability, and the senior executives *must* be kept informed, as they are responsible for decisions and actions taken. Only by acting on full information can correct decisions be made. We do not have access to all information provided to senior executives, just as other departments are not privy to all information about the surveillance room.

Consider how you would feel if someone outside the department started moving your cameras around without telling you. Several of your game cameras are left focused in on slot areas, and you haven't been informed. Then someone asks you what happened on a game and you find the hardwired VCR has been recording a slot machine. Someone without correct knowledge interfered in your area of responsibility, made decisions about what should or should not be recorded, and left your tail hanging out in the breeze. Yet you are still responsible.

38.

Know Neighboring Command Channels

It is the responsibility of investigators and supervisors to understand and follow the command lines of departments we work with. Supervisors in other departments have the right to make the decisions regarding the activities of their own personnel. Just as important, supervisory personnel have the authority to act in situations where action is required.

For instance, a security officer does not have the authority to detain an individual, except in certain specific situations. Security dispatch cannot order that someone be detained or asked to leave. That authority resides in the security supervisors and security shift manager or in the managers in other departments such as slots or casino (pit). Therefore, there is no shortcut involved in reporting (for example), a slot-credit claimer to security dispatch. For effective action to be taken, such as an individual being asked to leave, a security supervisor has to make the decision.

Remember also that it is not within the authority of surveillance personnel to order action: we observe and report. It is vital that reports go to the correct positions, through proper channels. The responsibility for any action taken lies with the person to whom we report. Our duty ends with supplying information to the correct people, through correct channels.

Effective reporting of information must include correct choice of speed of report (i.e., emergency versus routine) as well as correct routing.

Surveillance investigators and supervisors who bypass chain of command are actually, whether intentionally or not, sabotaging the effectiveness of all of our work. Incorrect reporting calls all reports into question and damages the reputation of our surveillance room. Without a reputation of effectiveness, none of our work does any good, as all reports will tend to be either questioned or ignored altogether.

Therefore, bypassing the chain of command carries the same penalties as false reporting. Bypassing chain of command, done unnecessarily, requires a warning. Habitual or intentional bypassing of chain of command is a termination offense, whether within the department or outside it. Intentionally keeping one's supervisor ignorant of information pertaining to casino surveillance is a termination offense.

39.

Direction of Attention[10]

In a surveillance room, the attention of operators and investigators most properly is focused outward. When attention of the eyes and mind is directed inward, toward the surveillance room and its people, personnel troubles result. People play political games. The casino itself is neglected.

Operators properly should be watching games, slots, cage, hard count, change booths, pits, and monitoring the activities of security. The only inward attention for surveillance investigators is ensuring that equipment is working properly and that logs and reports are correctly done.

Surveillance supervisors need to keep a minority of their attention reserved for activities within the room. Part of their job is ensuring that the investigators are doing their jobs and keeping their attention outward on the casino. They share the responsibility with the director of seeing that the equipment covers all areas of/or concern. They make recommendations on matters of scheduling, additional equipment needed, repairs, etc.

However, even the supervisors must keep the greatest majority of their attention directed outward. The supervisors are responsible for liaison with security, slot, cage, and pit management and for communications with the casino management in the absence of the director.

When investigators and operators focus their attention on the others in the surveillance room, on the people of the other shifts, rivalries, and other internal concerns, actual surveillance is being neglected. Minor errors such as a tape not rewound, a missing tape-log entry, etc., should simply be handled and dropped. More major errors, such as hardwired cameras being left off live games or information incorrectly disseminated, are the concern of the supervisors but should still be handled with a minimum of internal attention and correction. It is much more important to handle the problem than to find out who did it. A general notice to staff regarding a problem is just as effective as a heavy internal investigation, and it keeps the department's attention focused outward.

---

[10]Permission to reproduce obtained from the author, Jim Goding.

40.

Ethics Immunity[11]

People who do a good job have ethics protection.

When someone is not doing a good job—is not a valuable asset to the company—supervisors are very interested in every off-color activity, every single transgression of any minor rule.

A person who does a good job is defined as one who handles his responsibilities well and gets things done. In a surveillance room, this person has the games up on the monitors, watches the games, and watches the other areas of responsibility such as slots, cage, and count rooms. He or she sees the violations of procedures and any illegal activity and reports on it in such a way that action can be taken by the executives who receive the reports.

This also means that the person watching is able to see outpoints where he or she is looking and is able to write coherent reports that state exactly what happened. It means that the person knows enough about what he or she is supposed to be looking at and knows when something is not right.

People who have ethics protection show major personal responsibility in many ways, and the first of these is that they know their job and do it well. They don't let personal concerns distract them when they are at work. And usually, people who have ethics protection do not need it: people with that level of responsibility don't normally do things that they can be hit for. However, for people who do an outstanding job, little things are of no account. They can eat three meals a day off the company; office supplies can disappear from their desks; they can show up a little late for work; and they can get unauthorized overtime. Because the bosses know that they are doing their jobs well, the little bits of extra cost are of no account.

However, there is also a down side to this. If such people should take a downturn in their performance, the executives are very interested. What is happening? Are they suddenly getting involved in something crooked? Such an activity would make them tend to lose interest in keeping the company's interests in mind.

---

[11]Permission to reproduce obtained from the author, Jim Goding.

When people's performance starts slacking off, their supervisors should be very interested, no matter the reason. If they have suddenly started pilfering the till, so to speak, their supervisors want to know. Maybe they can turn them around before these excellent performers pass a point of no return. Maybe it's overwhelming personal problems, and sometimes a simple talk with the boss can help. However, if their performance continues to slide, they lose their ethics protection.

There is one more part of this that should be noted: A report of a transgression against a person who does a good job, who puts 100 percent into the job, should be viewed with suspicion by the supervisor who receives the report. Who filed the report? Is that person doing a good job, or is the person simply trying to get someone in trouble in order to distract attention from his or her own off-color, out-ethics activity or lack of activity? Is the report true? Or is it simply vitriol, put out by someone who should be under investigation?

This also applies to the work of the surveillance room. Are the reports being done merely to keep the attention of the executives off the reporter? Is that floor person actually doing his or her job and the isolated incident just that? Is the dealer or cashier someone who in fact is a major asset to the company? Is this dealer one that brings hundreds of people back to the casino, or is he or she, as the "report" states, someone who is rude, sloppy, never clears his hands, and actively drives people off his table? Is information given to the surveillance room true, or is it passed on to surveillance merely to keep their attention elsewhere while the till is being robbed? Executives should take these things into consideration, and so should the surveillance people who observe and report.

41.

Dealing With the General Manager[12]

The most important thing to remember in dealing with general managers of casinos is that they hate to waste their time and energy.

This means that you really don't want to do things twice. If you don't follow the pointers below, your work will almost always have to be redone, with considerable irritation to the general manager.

1. Make sure you have your facts straight. Verify information from sources not within your control.

2. Put it in writing.

3. Never present conclusions or opinions as fact.

4. Include all pertinent facts, even if they do not support your conclusions. Information not included, and noticed by an executive, reduces your credibility.

5. Do not include information that has nothing to do with the presentation in any presentation.

6. Attempt to account for all information. If there is data that is not accounted for, point out this fact.

7. Don't take it personally if your conclusions are not accepted. It is highly likely that the general manager has information or has to deal with things that you don't know about.

8. Leave the legal-eagle angles to the specialists. Simply present your facts and conclusions, and proposals if applicable.

9. Remember that proposals to spend money must result in increased ability to either create revenue or save the company money. Legal requirements should be bolstered by ability to create revenue.

---

[12]Permission to reproduce obtained from the author, Jim Goding.

10. Never ask for the minimum required.

When all is said and done, the most important thing in dealing with superiors is that they must be able to trust you and take you at your word. This means that no falsehood of any kind should be used in your dealing with your superiors.

42.

Politics[13]

Basic rule: The surveillance department does not become involved in company or corporate politics.

Basic Principle 1: Any member of the organization that attacks or attempts to neutralize a trained and effective surveillance department has something that he or she wishes to hide.

Basic Principle 2: When a surveillance department becomes involved in political games, either internally or with other areas of the company or greater corporation, its attention has been effectively directed away from its proper focus.

Basic Principle 3: When someone outside the department attempts to involve surveillance in political squabbles, he or she is attempting to neutralize the department.

These principles apply as well to any other department (security, audits) whose job it is to locate and handle theft or dishonesty.

Surveillance managers and staff should look with a good deal of skepticism upon any reports, especially verbal reports, of generalities about other areas of the organization.

The surveillance department deals in specifics: events with personnel, time, and location. While it is true that it is our purpose to investigate and document events, it can be very distracting to hear a verbal report that "someone told me that there is a dealer on swing or graveyard that is paying people too much."

---

[13]Permission to reproduce obtained from the author, Jim Goding.

43.

Attacks on Surveillance Personnel

When the manager or supervisors in a surveillance department come under attack from inside or outside the department, realize that one of three things is occurring:

1. In an attack originating within the department, someone has formed an alliance outside the department with someone who is hiding something.

2. In an attack from outside the department, someone is attempting to distract attention away from him- or herself.

3. The personnel under attack may actually be at fault.

These three things should all be investigated. However, those doing the investigation should first look at who is being attacked. If this person is one of the most effective members of the department, the likelihood is that the attack is an attempt to neutralize surveillance or even to make that person, specifically, ineffective because of suspicion. The director should find out what is known, and direct the investigation accordingly.

Section B:
Slots

44.

The Tells of External Theft and Cheating[14]

There are numerous ways to cheat a slot machine. It is safe to say that there is not a slot machine out there today that cannot be or will not be cheated some-time.

We are going to go over a few basic cheating techniques:

1. Slugs

2. Counterfeit coins

3. Devices used to disrupt coin readers

4. Shaved tokens

5. Professional play on slot machines

6. Opening the machines and injecting random access memory (RAM) with false information

7. Breaking into the area that houses the money

8. Stuffing items into the coin chutes

9. Manipulation of the play buttons

10. Crimes in and within around the slot machines such as distracting grabs

11. The short-change artist.

There are also the internal theft avenues regarding the slots area:

1. Shorting of customers

2. Cashier and change person theft

3. False fills to the machine

4. False jackpots.

---

[14]Permission to reproduce obtained from the author, Derk Boss.

The start to basic cheating slot techniques is with slugs. Slugs, on a normal basis, are dollar-sized lead tokens. A slug, when made correctly, fools the coin accepter housed in the machine, letting the machine know that it is a good token. Here are the indicators of someone using slugs:

1. Playing out of his pockets. Obviously this person is not going to come into the casino and purchase tokens from a change person or change booth.

2. Separation or sorting of coin or tokens from a bucket or other pockets.

3. Rubbernecking: constantly looking around to see if he or she is being watched.

4. Blockers: another person standing right beside the machine to block view of the actions.

5. Coins or tokens frequently falling through into the payout tray.

Detection and Prevention Techniques

1. Consistent surveillance of the slot areas.

2. Investigation of suspicious players or activity. This requires good communi-cation between the slot departments, security, and surveillance.

3. Establish dedicated coverage for those areas being hit. This is also a pre-ventive measure. Camera presence does deter.

4. Review working monitor tapes and others for suspects in the areas being hit.

Slugs look different. They are dull, normally gray in color, and there are no serrated edges on the sides of the tokens. Most tokens are made from molds that you pour hot lead into.

A good way to link slugs to a particular individual or individuals is that "finger-prints" appear on the slugs, meaning a map of the same mold, over and over; so if there is a certain crack in the mold, it will appear in the lead. So if there is a slug on top of the coins housed in the lower drop area, a slug on top of the other coins in the hopper, a slug stuck in the coin accepter, and one in the subject's pocket, and all of these have the same mold characteristics, probable cause leads us to believe that all of the slugs came from the same person and were possibly manufactured by that same individual.

45.

Slot Slugger Profile[15]

The primary reason a person will slug a slot machine is to gain a profit from their act. Although an even exchange profit is the primary reason for slugging, not all sluggers will slug a machine and leave with a profit, even though the slugging act produced a profit. The professional slot cheat is not a slugger. The slugger is usually a petit thief or drug user. The person who manufactures slugs will generate a hundred to five hundred slugs at a time, and then sell them at 10 to 50 cents on the dollar depending on the market. The slugger can be anyone. Do not stereotype the slugger. The slugger can be young, old, male, female, well dressed or not. So how can the slugger be detected? The following are indicators of a possible slugger:

● Watch for the slugger playing out of his hand. (Although this is the most common, sluggers have been known to rack their slugs, roll the slugs, and even buy tokens from a change person to cover their act.)

● Watch for the slugger using one hand to feed the slugs into the machine and the other hand in the tray to catch the slugs if they fall through. The slug makes a very unique sound when it hits the tray. When on the casino floor, this is something you should be aware of in detecting the slugger.

● Watch for the slugger testing machines. The slugger will be seen going from machine to machine until a machine accepts the slugs.*

● Watch for the slugs falling through the machine.*

● Watch for the separation of the tokens from the slugs.*

● Watch for tokens (slugs) being taken from pockets (pants, jacket, purses, fanny packs, etc.).*

● Watch for blockers: Persons who stand to either side of the slugger for the purpose of protecting the slugger from detection.

● Watch for persons who have a coin bucket or other container in their lap with their arm or something over the container to conceal the slugs.

---

[15]Reproduced with permission from Al Bentley, *SINdicate* 2 (March 2001).

- Watch for slow play with rubber necking (movement of the head in a searching manner; appears to be looking for someone, like an employee who might detect their actions).

- Watch for tokens (slugs) being received from someone else. The carrier (person with the slugs) is also the lookout or blocker. If detected, this person is the first to leave so if the slugger is stopped, they won't be in possession of the slugs.

- Watch for short play with a cash out. The slugger normally will play only enough to receive a small profit from their slugs, then move to another machine. This is not always true; some who have gambling problems will play until they lose everything. This player can be at a machine for long periods and will be seen playing credits, which is uncommon with sluggers.

*These are very important points of evidence in the prosecution of this gaming crime.

46.

Slot investigations[16]

For years the slot area was not an area of major concern for the casino. Now in the twenty-first century the slot area has been identified as a major, potential area for losses. Today with more sophisticated ways of circumventing the safeguards of slot machines, surveillance must also learn and utilize all the information available to them in their investigations of slot-related crimes.

What are the most useful keys that surveillance departments can utilize in their investigations? Time—Location—Method—Pattern

How can we determine when the incident happened (Time)? The first is the eyewitness, who can establish the time and location by his presence in the area. But most of the time evidence is found after the crime has been committed. In those cases we must rely on information available from the slot department and the machine(s) itself.

First determine who were the last employees to enter the machine prior to the incident. We like to have at least two employees at a time enter a machine. You can keep track in two ways. One, the Machine Entry Access Log (MEAL) is a book maintained inside the machine that the employees who enter the machine are required to sign. This will give you information on fills or maintenance checks like jams and machine time-outs. The other is a printout from the slot tracking system. If requested, the machine(s) can be isolated to an approximate date and time and the printout will indicate who placed a card into the machine's tracking system, both employee(s) and patron(s). Then a printout of the machine(s) coin-in, coin-out activity can be obtained. With this information you can see which employee(s) entered the machine(s) and verify it against MEAL to see if someone is trying to conceal their entry.

Also, the video coverage can be matched to the same time line of the events at the machine to also determine if anyone was trying to conceal their entry. In regard to identifying a possible patron who was cheating the machine(s), the same information will eliminate most of the subjects at the machine(s). The coin-in and coin-out, matched against the player tracking report, will establish a time-line of activity of which subjects were using a Slot Club card and which were not. (Most subjects who cheat a machine do not register with your slot club.)

---

[16]Reproduced with permission from Al Bentley, *SINdicate* 2 (February 2001).

Also the coin-in and coin-out report can help identify unusual activity. Example: The slot department reports finding slugs in three machines in the amounts of 3, 23, and 10. From the report you can see during an hour period on these three machines you have coin-in activity, which closely matches the slugs found in each machine. Also at this time the Slot Club card was not used. With this information you can feel confident that you have a possible suspect. Then with the use of the video coverage, a suspect can be identified. Once the suspect has been identified and returns, and is observed using slugs, then the suspect can be arrested and the prior information can be used against the suspect in your case.

In the past these types of reports could tie up surveillance personnel for days reviewing video coverage. This same type of information can be obtained with regard to other slot investigations: suspicious jackpots, suspicious marking in machine(s), suspicious employee activity, and unusual or low hold variances.

47.

Slot Investigations— The Method and Pattern[17]

The Method

The method is how the slot machine is being cheated. Let us take a minute to look at a few of the methods of cheating slot machines.

The most common is slugging a slot machine, the use of manufactured lead tokens. These tokens can be as crude as a token-shaped slugs without any design to camouflage the slugs. The more sophisticated slugs have a design on one or both sides. All these types of slugs are manufactured by sand casting a real casino token: pressing a real casino token into a sand-cast to form the shape and design of the token. These casts can manufacture several slug tokens at a time by pouring lead into the sand cast molds.

There are also shaved tokens. These are actual casino tokens altered to be accepted as credits into a machine, but not counted as a coin out in the payout. An example of this is when the cheater feeds in ten shaved tokens into a machine and receives ten credits. When the cheater cashes out the credits, he receives ten casino tokens plus the ten shaved tokens. This is repeated until only shaved tokens are in the payout, because all the casino tokens have been emptied from the hopper. This is an example, not an exact scenario.

Today, in addition to the slugs described above, slugs are being manufactured by methods as sophisticated as the tokens legally manufactured for casinos. These slugs are considered counterfeits. Counterfeit tokens are manufactured like a jeweler would manufacture a medallion, by forming a cast from real casino tokens. The difference is that the lead compound is poured into the cast, then a high-speed centrifuge will force the compound into the cast so that all the details of the token cast are an exact copy of the token used. Most of the slot machines today will not take these tokens. But because they are so good in quality, they are being cashed in at the change booths, with change personnel and at casino cages.

In addition to slugs, the cheaters have found different ways of interrupting the optic device on slot machines. The optic-device is what counts the tokens leaving the slot machine. The optic-device tools used by cheaters either block or interrupt the optic counter in the slot machine. This allows for additional tokens to be received by the cheater in the payouts. There are many other

---

[17]Reproduced with permission from Al Bentley, *SINdicate* 2 (May 2001).

cheating devices, but for the most part they are used to receive additional tokens in the payout.

How can this knowledge help the surveillance department catch these cheaters? We now know the Method and we want to find the Pattern. Using the player tracking reports, the coin-in and coin-out reports, along with the standard questions we should ask about any slugs found in the machines, will establish the Pattern.

Remember these questions: Where were the slugs, on the top of the hopper or in the drop? Was the diverter opened to the hopper or the drop?

What do these questions tell you? Well, it's about time. If the slugs are on the top of the hopper, then the last couple of players are likely to be your subject. If the slugs are mixed, then you may have to look further back. But if the slugs are in the drop, then you may have to go back as far as the last drop. What about the diverter? What does the diverter tell you? If the diverter is open to the hopper, look at the last few players. When the diverter is open to the drop, you have to look for slugs in the hopper and the drop. If no slugs are found in the hopper, then it must be handled as if the slugs were only in the drop. Remember, if you believe someone is slugging a machine and when the machine's hopper is checked no slugs are found, the diverter is probably open to the drop and not the hopper.

The Pattern

What patterns are we looking for? The first is method: are they slugging, passing counterfeit tokens or using a cheating device like an optic device? Can the evidence lead us to someone? Are the slugs all alike, manufactured in the same molds? Are there different patterns on the slugs? This likeness can tie a slug or device to a known manufacturer or person.

The second pattern is location: Where are the machines being cheated? What kind of slot machines are being cheated? Where are the tokens being cashed out—change booths, cage cashiers or change personnel on the floor? Where were the cheating devices found? Did the slot technicians find any markings that were made by the cheating devices?

Once the above information is known, then it is time to gather supporting information from the slot department. On each machine where activity has occurred, a slot technician should run the machine's history. The history will tell you the coin-in and coin-out activity, any coin payouts which were interrupted and any jackpots paid out during the period in which you have stated. It is very important to establish a time period to work between. The shorter the time period, the better information will be. Other reports that will assist you are the Machine Entry Access Log (MEAL) and the player tracking activity reports on those machines.

48.

Shaved Tokens

There are a few other ways to fool the coin accepter or the payout counter in a slot machine. One of these is known as shaved tokens.

Most newer machines contain an optic sensor that counts the coins paid out. Every time a coin passes through that optic sensor, it breaks the beam. Every time a coin breaks the beam it counts a coin as being paid out.

Coins can be shaved so that they do not break the light beam, and are thus not counted as being paid out. So, we have a properly working machine and we have 100 shaved quarters and a number of real quarters in the hopper of the machine. The cheater deposits those 100 quarters, builds up 100 credits, and then cashes out. The machine will count out 100 good quarters and also put out the shaved quarters, without them being counted.

The major tell for catching people who use these shaved coins or tokens is that they have to sort the coins, keeping the shaved coins in one area and the legitimate coins in another. Rubbernecking is again a very good indicator, looking around to see if anyone is watching what's going on around them. Also look out for people using blockers (co-conspirators). The coins will frequently fall through the trays, not being accepted, and you can hear this as you are walking by. The coin-out counter obviously would not meet the win meter, so you can see more coins being paid out than are registered on the win meter. Also look for frequent cash-out of credits from the machine, in other words, someone keeps loading it up and instantly cashing it out. They are doing this not to play the machine but to receive more coins back. Shaved tokens are found in the drop during the weigh or the wrap, they are an indicator that someone has been cheating that machine. Many suspects will cash tokens immediately as they are paid out of the machine. The normal occasional player or tourist will hold onto the coin and walk through the casino, or maybe save it in a bucket for the next day.

The best procedures against the use of shaved tokens is to have an excellent rapport with your hard-count department and other slot personnel, who would report any unusual-size coins or tokens, or different denominations of token in a machine. (For example, a fifty-peso coin may fit a one-dollar machine.) Any odd coin found in the hopper or drop should be reported to surveillance.

It is good if a slot department is able to report to you when a machine has been receiving an out-of-ordinary amount of fills, such as three within an eight-hour period.

49.

Detection Techniques

It takes total teamwork from other departments to properly protect your machines. Some detection techniques for the shaved coins or tokens:

1.   Observe rubberneckers.

2.   Determine a reason for an unusual number of fills for a particular machine.

3.   Investigate reports of unusual size coins.

4.   Check out players who frequently cash out coin or credits, and check the payout meter against reel symbols for correct pays.

5.   Make sure the machine is maintained correctly; you may just have an over payer.

50.

Counterfeit Tokens

Counterfeit token are made with only the finest machinery and stamps or a cast and centrifuge that jewelers would use. They are made in very fine detail, as if they were actually counterfeiting a U.S. silver dollar. This type of venture is very expensive for the counterfeiter, so you will find most counterfeit tokens in the upper areas, in the one-, five- , twenty-five-, and hundred-dollar slot machines.

A lot of times the counterfeit tokens will be rejected and fall through; that would be one of the tells. Someone putting maximum coins in and then cashing out credits immediately with minimal play, or on-and-off play, you need to look at more closely. Again, a major tell is looking around, rubbernecking.

This type of crime is usually done with a number of people and is very well and highly organized. They often come in from another state; they have teams that work for only a short time, being very careful not to overload one particular area. A good procedure is to know at all times what your token inventory is. Obviously, if you have a set amount of token inventory you are able to determine if there is an overage. Maintain dedicated CCTV coverage of all high-action slots, coverage of high-action players, coverage of fills and jackpots in those areas.

Some detection techniques include routinely checking high-action players, monitoring all unknown high-action players, and determining if there was a reason for hopper fills and what the reason was.

Remember that these people are highly organized. They have spent a lot of money for the presses and spin casting to make these tokens. They are not going to sacrifice such an expensive investment by getting caught, so they are very careful and shrewd.

51.

Counterfeit Money

The next step up from counterfeit tokens would be counterfeit bills of U.S. currency. These types of bills can be placed in a bill validator, the device which allows players to enter cash into the slot machine for credits.

Counterfeit money is very hard to detect these days. It is easy to get change from change personnel, from change booths, or actually from the machine itself.

Always be on the lookout for frequent inputs of cash and frequent cash-out of credits, minimal or brief playing, quick hits, and the player or an associate of the slot player continuously at the cage or booth cashing out. Check out unknown players in your high-limit area. Observe or review video when bills are being rejected often; a lot of times the suspect will try to insert the bill in the bill validator a number of times.

A counterfeiter, just like a person with a shaved token or counterfeit token, will keep the money separate, bills from the bill validator in one location and bills from the cash-out to another location.

Some good procedures against the use of counterfeit money are to investigate reports of all suspected counterfeit bills found in the bill-validator units. Review dedicated coverage to any machines where bad bills have been found. Review all existing tape on change booths to try to link any suspects to different areas of the casino and to that machine.

52.

Cheating Bill Validators

There are also methods for cheating the bill validator itself other than using counterfeit money. There have been several ways that individuals have attempted to defraud machines by actions taken on the bill validator itself.

1. For example, the person sees player put a twenty-dollar bill into the bill validator and lose and walk away. He or she then goes to the machine with some type of high-powered radio signal, like walkie-talkie, and keys it in front of the bill validator a number of times until it goes into a time-out mode and starts blinking.

2. Another way to put a bill validator into a time-out mode would be to enter into it some type of card with a magnetic strip. Once the bill validator goes into a time-out mode, the person very quietly waits for a slot attendant and tells the attendant he or she put twenty dollars into the machine but did not receive any credits. On a normal basis, the slot mechanic or floor person will look into the machine, see that a twenty-dollar bill was the last one entered into the bill validator, and will give the subject the twenty dollars in credits.

3. There have also been cheating techniques where a bill was attached to strings on each side, or with holes in the bill in key locations; the bill validator accepts it and adds up the credits and then the bill is pulled out. A commonly used substance for tying onto the bill is dental floss, which is taped with transparent tape to one side of a $100 bill. The string is on the outside edge, forming a loop off the back end of the bill. The bill would be inserted into the bill validator until the credits are registered, but is held up from being sent into the moneybox by the loop at the back of the end of the bill, which is being held by the subject. Then a piece of plastic slightly smaller than the bill is inserted into the bill validator, lying directly under the bill. Once the plastic is inserted and lined up under the entire bill, the bill validator rejects the plastic and both the plastic and the bill are pulled out together.

53.

Disruption of Coin Readers

Optic Devices

A common device used to disrupt coin readers is called an *optic device*. Within a slot machine, there are a number of areas that are checked by using optic lighting sensors, such as size of coin, coin-in, and coin-out. The way they work is, for example, if somebody has twenty credits on a slot machine and pushes "cash-out," the hopper starts turning and feeding the coins up through the area to the payout chute. Every time a coin passes through the light beam, it disrupts the beam—breaks its connection—which registers the coin on the counter. When twenty coins come out, the optics have counted twenty coins and the hopper quits paying coins out to the customer.

Basically, an optic device used for cheating would be a small "wheat-grain" light bulb, which is placed into the machine, usually through the coin payout chute. It will slide right up next to the sensor that reads the beam to count the coins. The cheater pushes "cash-out," the coins circumvent and go past the device and the beam is never broken and the hopper will keep paying out coins. When these devices are used in the machines, they can only be used in eight- to ten-second intervals, or the machine will go into a time-out from another protective device in the machine that tells when coins are not being counted.

One tell that the device has or is being used on your machines is that the coin payout meter does not match the coin paid out or if the payout does not match the symbols on the real—e.g., the jackpot is for five dollars but you know it just paid out twenty. Or the hoppers on your machines are found empty or nearly empty without players present, or you know through your paper trail they haven't had high-end play.

You will see a player reach up into the payout chute to place the device or to retrieve it out of the machine.

These types of devices are usually used on higher-denomination machines such as one dollar, five dollar, and twenty-five dollar and above, but I have seen them used on machines all the way down to quarters and nickels.

A lot of times there will be people around the suspect, coconspirators, to block the view of the action of the device being put in and out.

Some procedures against the use of this type of a device start with proper training of slot personnel. They should approach all new, unknown players on high-denomination machines. Slot personnel should immediately report an unusual amount of fills to a specific machine. All reports should be investigated. Investigate reports of unattended machines with empty or nearly empty hoppers. Good detection techniques include reviewing the tapes to identify all suspects.

One should dedicate coverage to high-denomination areas. This is a good visual deterrent and provides a good video trail to catch the culprit. Have a good rapport with security and slot personnel to keep a constant patrol roving through those areas of high-limit machines.

All large jackpots in the high-limit area should be investigated by a complete review on tape. A procedure against any type of cheating on a high-denomination machine, whether it is by optic device or by injecting the RAM with false information, would be to hold all large jackpots until surveillance can review all tapes completely. When reviewing the tape, look for blockers or distracters or any unusual activity around the machine that your normal, everyday player would not be doing, or in areas that they wouldn't be going to.

One thing that you should do right off the top to protect any property is to ensure that all slot machines with large jackpots and progressive-type slot machines have dedicated unobstructed coverage, so that when an incident or a big win does occur, you can review a thorough tape.

One thing to look for, and a most obvious way to steal or cheat a slot machine, is to break into the drop door or actually enter the machine to extract coins from the drop bucket or hopper or bill validator. An indication that this may be going on would be an illegal drop-door-open signal at an unusual time of day, with or without notification from the slot department. Look for suspicious individuals loitering around the drop areas, not really playing the machines but paying more attention to the locks. If you see an unsecured or broken door or lock on the machines, this is an indication that something may have gone wrong, or it may be a co-conspiracy with employees, as is the case when a drop crew leaves behind a drop bucket or validator, especially if it is "hot"(meaning it contains money).

A good procedure against breaking into machines is, to start with, to put a washer around the lock so that even if someone were to grab it and turn it, it would just spin around the lock. Most drop doors are made from pressed wood, and the locks are very easy to pull out or unscrew. You can also use a recessed drop-door lock.

Maintain good drop security. It is a very good idea for the slot department (or any other department on the casino floor) to immediately report any broken dropped door or any suspicious circumstances or individuals. Slots personnel must strictly monitor slot data systems for drop alarms.

Always be on the lookout. Look for suspicious moves, people carrying tools in their hands around lock areas, a lot of people gathering around a machine, and rubbernecking.

If you see a door open on a machine, you know that the light on the top of the machine (known as a *candle*) should be on. There is a technique for covering that candle with a larger candle that blocks out the light. It just slips right over it.

54.

Stuffed Coin Chutes

Another simple way of stealing from the machine is to stuff the coin chute. You can stuff the coin chute with paper or a magnet. This causes short payouts; patrons lose some coins in the coin return or in the payout. Suspects must reach up into the coin chute to remove the material and coins, and again the people will be looking around, rubbernecking. People who stuff a machine usually walk around the casino with no particular goal in mind; they just appear to wander about the slot areas, and of course they will rarely play. When they pull out whatever they stuffed the chute with, the coins that they have caught will fall out—coins that belonged to the patrons before them.

Procedures against this type of activity, of course, are good communication between the slots, security, and surveillance departments. Slot personnel should check for blockages upon receiving reports of partial or short pays. Security and slot departments should report individuals acting suspiciously to surveillance, to security, and to their supervisors. Everyone needs to be on the lookout, as total teamwork. This involves monitoring slot areas for subjects casing or loitering about, looking for particular payouts, looking for credits. These types of people should be reported immediately to security and surveillance.

If you have an individual who comes into your property quite often and just seems to loiter and walk around about the machines taking credits here and there, I would say that the best defense is to have the person legally removed from your property, so they cannot return. This eliminates any possibility of theft from your patrons, who are the most important entity to your business.

Short-Change Artist

There is an area that not a lot of people think of as a theft from your slot department, but it is: the simple short-change artist. This type of person will attempt to confuse your cashier or change person with more than one type of transaction at a time. One good way to prevent this is right within your internal controls: make sure that the employees perform and complete one transaction at a time. These people should also be trained to know the indicators of a scam artist; they can then get on their communication and notify a supervisor immediately upon any suspicious activity or attempted multiple transactions.

Once you determine that a short-change was attempted, you should immediately run back video surveillance tapes and attempt to get photos of the individual and see that the photos are circulated throughout your security and slot departments. Short-change artists are very good at what they do. A good short-change artist can take advantage of your best casino worker.

Proper communication between departments, training, and a good state-of-the-art surveillance room are your best deterrents. There are many cheating devices out there that used to work, that don't work, or that may work such as clickers, slant-top manipulators, kick stands, optics for uprights, optics for slant tops, shims, wires, monkey paws. They all have nicknames. They all work sometimes and there always will be devices that work.

Our past experiences have shown that even before a slot machine is out on a test run on a casino floor, it is already in somebody's garage being disassembled. The criminals have analyzed it and know how to cheat it every which way, and are just waiting for that machine to be put on the floor. Just remember, when it comes to cheating a slot machine, there is not a slot machine made that can't be cheated.

The way we learn about slot cheating methods usually is not from the person who buys that machine or invents the device. A device may be used for six months and then sold on the street. The buyer is the person who gets arrested, and this is how we learn about different slot cheating devices.

So right now, as you are reading this book, there are many people and many devices out there that we don't have a clue about. They are out there cheating our machines and there is nothing we can do about it until we detect it. Again, dedicated camera coverage and good liaison and communication between related departments are proven formulas for catching cheaters.

55.

Internal Theft: False Hopper Fills

False Hopper Fills: Tells

1. Fill slip is not signed at the location of the fill.

2. Coin for fill is not placed directly into the hopper.

3. The correct signature of verifying personnel may not be legible or identifiable on the fill slip.

4. The fill is not located at the machine listed on the slot system or paper trail.

5. The required number of personnel are not present at the fill.

6. Fill bag had been opened prior to arriving at the machine.

False Hopper Fills: Procedures for Prevention

Dedicated closed circuit television (CCTV) coverage: Know what the slot fill procedures are so that when your surveillance department is observing a fill, you know when a procedure is broken.

It helps if surveillance is notified of fills on all high-denomination machines for verification; hopefully they will also have a security officer present during that type of fill. A good tool for surveillance that would possibly lead to revealing false hopper fills is to investigate any machine that has an excess of three fills in a twenty-four-hour period.

The best way to detect these things is, of course, to audit fill procedures routinely and consistently. Have good, dedicated CCTV coverage and know what the procedures are.

False Jackpots: Key Indicators

1. The jackpot form is not signed at the location of the jackpot.

2. Jackpot is not located at the machine listed on the slot monitoring system or your paper trail.

3. The required number of personnel are not present at the jackpot for all the appropriate paperwork.

4. Signatures of verifying personnel are not legible or are unidentifiable.

Know and strictly enforce all slot jackpot procedures. Surveillance should be notified of large jackpots for verification. This is where your dedicated CCTV cameras come in, because you can verify play and the amount of coins put in as well as reel alignment. One of the best detection techniques is to audit jackpot procedures routinely and consistently through a CCTV system, as well as through a paper trail.

56.

Cashier or Change Person Theft

A key area to watch for internal theft is from your cashiers and change persons. Some indicators that a theft of this type may be occurring are

1. An employee goes to the body or the pockets or other areas without clearing their hands.

2. An incoming cashier discovers short straps of currency positioned in the back of the drawer.

3. The relieving cashier doesn't count down the bank and accepts the number that the off-going cashier gives him or her.

4. An employee counts down the bank numerous times.

5. Constantly counting or manipulating the funds in the bank possibly misplacing bills, like a twenty-dollar bill under a stack of five-dollar bills.

6. Rolls of coins are missing out of the cans, but are then later discovered placed behind other cans.

7. The change person is constantly looking around or appears very aware of where the surveillance cameras are and tries to block the views.

Cashier or Change Person Theft: Prevention

1. Strictly prohibit unauthorized count-down of the bank.

2. Make sure that the balance of the bank is in fact correct by a complete countdown by the incoming and off-going employee.

3. Make sure that all coin bags are weighed and completely investigate any shortages.

One good method of detection is for an actual slot manager to monitor cashiers and change personnel frequently, by signing out videotapes and reviewing them in the surveillance room. Monitor and investigate cashiers, change personnel, or any one else who seems to display any of the above-listed tells. Fully and totally investigate all shortages, leaving no stone unturned.

57.

Thefts From Coin Machines

Trusted employees such as slot technicians and slot supervisors occasionally steal directly from the machines. A good tell that something may be going on is a floor person or technician who enters a machine for no apparent reason or without a player present. During this entry you notice that they do not sign the repair log or the entry log within the machine. While the machine is open you see hands to the body without clearing them for the camera—in other words, moves to the pockets.

The best procedure against this type of theft is using a good closed circuit television (CCTV) surveillance system and requiring employees to clear their hands after entering the machine or before touching the body. Let them know you can see this on film. This also sublimely lets the person know that when they are going into a machine and the right people are not there or they are not seen clearing their hands, they will be questioned.

It is a good idea to require all personnel who enter machines to use a system card and sign an entry card, as mentioned earlier. The best and only way to detect this type of theft is to monitor the floor and technical personnel on a routine basis. Again, a slot shift manager or above signing out tapes from the surveillance room and actually reviewing at random certain key shots such as aisles, would show unauthorized entry into a machine.

Section C:
Crimes Against the Patrons
Within the Casino

58.

Crimes Against Patrons Within the Casino

The most valuable entity on the floor is the casino patron, not the slot machine or the 21 table. You must always provide a safe and healthy environment for your customers. Here are some definite tells that you may see from thieves on your casino floor who have your patrons as targets.

Individuals will enter the casino as a group and then split up, moving in the same direction but parallel to one another or one behind the other. These individuals will stick out, because they tend to roam the slot areas without actually playing.

Your patrons—the ones that are playing the machines—are usually enthralled or concentrating on the slot machine and not watching what is going on around them. This is where security comes in; to protect the guests and pick out the people who may be thieves or cause harm to the patrons.

Individuals who roam the slot areas without playing will often carry coins in their hands or coin buckets. They will work as a team or sometimes individually; one person will throw a coin to the right of a slot player, tossing the coin toward the metal base of the player's chair. When the patron hears the sound, he turns around and bends over to pick up the coin, thinking that he or she dropped the coin. The bucket or rack of coin the patron is using is sitting on the other side, and of course the coconspirator will grab the bucket while the patron is distracted by picking up the dropped coin. This is called a distract-and-grab.

There are also teams that will actually engage the customer in conversation. For instance, a man-and-woman team: a woman would approach another woman, getting her to turn her back to where she is keeping her coin handy, the "distracter," and may ask the patron to close a clasp on her watch; while the patron is doing that, the coconspirator is relieving the patron of her money.

One must always keep in mind that when one of your customers has something stolen from them—especially money—they are going to tell another person, and that person will tell another. On an average you will probably lose ten customers who would have normally come to your property; they will go elsewhere because of this story of theft.

59.

Distract and Grab: Prevention

When individuals are seen roaming through the slot area not playing, and when you determine that they are not just a lost customer, and they are there for no other reason than to prey on your guests, have them formally charged with trespassing and removed from your property.

Put on a good training program for your slot and security personnel as well as your surveillance personnel, including anyone involved on the floor, to train them to recognize these types of people. A surveillance department cannot do it all on its own, without the teamwork of a well trained security, slot department and other employees. Train your employees how to approach and greet the subjects, or to report them to surveillance or security.

There is no reason for anyone to get hurt because someone relieved one of your patrons of their money. Everyone loses in this situation if a suspect is not approached correctly.

A good closed crcuit television (CCTV) system recording fixed shots of main aisles throughout your slot department helps to pick out, or bring to the attention of your personnel, when someone is just roaming the casino.

Good communication between surveillance and security via radio will, in fact, be a deterrent to these criminal teams, as well as an aid in successfully protecting your patrons.

If an unfortunate incident occurs—one of your patrons has money or items stolen from them—just review the tapes of the area in their entirety and from as many different angles as you can. Look for the suspects entering the building without appearing to want to play, roaming the casino, and finding the target. Put the crime together in chronological order and write the report. Once you have your suspects identified, take numerous photos and get the photos out to the pertinent people in your own casino, other casinos, and police departments. Circulate fliers around your property. Keep the awareness going. Continue to be proactive.

60.

The Impersonator

Another type of theft against patrons is the person who comes in and imperson-ates an employee. For example, your shift managers or slot floor men person-nel wear blue jackets; an individual will obtain a blue jacket and wear it in the casino in order to blend in and create the impression of being an employee. Some impersonators go so far as actually having a mock name badge.

These people roam the casino floor and do not gamble, but pay more attention to the patrons. They prey on people who want change. They will approach a machine with the "change" light on and say, "May I help you?" The patron looks at them, with the nametag and the same color of jacket, and gives them a hundred dollars. The impersonator says, "I will be right back with your coin or your token," and then leaves the property. The patron is just left sitting while their money walks out the door. These people normally make a score and head for the door immediately. Good areas to look for suspects are those covered by your exit and entrance cameras, as well as your main-aisle cameras.

Training, training, training for all departments, and good communication and teamwork, will in most cases stop this type of crime from occurring. You have to train personnel on how to approach the individual and how to get them off the casino floor. Review all tapes, all angles, and all doors to put together a chrono-logical line of events of the crime or the attempt. Take photos, write the re-ports, and circulate all pertinent information both within your property and to other properties. Train your casino floor staff to report people they don't recog-nize that appear to be dressed liked one of your employees.

61.

Bonus Players

Another situation that occurs on the casino floor involves individuals known as *bonus players*. Although they don't steal from a patron, their actions fall into a gray area. Bonus players cause you to lose your customers. They prey on your patrons that play bonus-type machines. Certain machines build up bonus payouts, in addition to the normal jackpot payouts, for coins played or time played or for getting certain combinations of symbols. You get to a certain spot you push a button, and you get rewards from machines of that type. The bonus player will watch the patron play the machine for a couple of hours at a time, and when the bonus is getting ready to pay out, they will intimidate the person off the machine—blow smoke in their face, continuously bump into them, be obnoxious, or start an argument with the person playing the machine. They try to lure the person away from the machine and then they or a coconspirator moves in on that same machine.

Although they are not stealing from that individual, they are cashing in on the benefit of that person's play. If you have a customer who is treated rudely and obnoxiously by what appear to be other customers, and there is not a well trained staff member to deal with this type of activity and it is not deterred, you will lose that customer—and many more to follow, by word of mouth.

There is also what is called *team play*. Certain machines or banks of slot machines obtain high bonus ratings and provide some predictability: on an average one can tell when they are getting ready to hit. The teams will then come into your casino and take up every chair and every slot machine and play them until the bonus hits. This is good for the casino but it is very bad for your patrons. It is better to have your usual patrons and paying guests playing than some team that comes in only long enough to collect a predicted bonus or jackpot. What this actually does is stop your patron—the person that is staying with you—from playing and enjoying that machine or going for that bonus, because the team, who are usually locals, just lock it up.

Some casinos have gone to the extent of actually putting up signs that say, "No team play." There are advantages and disadvantages to regulating team play. For example, the graveyard shift at three or four in the morning has hardly anybody in the casino; some team players want to come in and play that bank of machines. You are, then, getting play on those machines, and this is better than those machines being idle. But during normal business hours—the day-time and the late evenings, all the way up to just past midnight—sometimes you still have a lot of customers in your casino. You have shows getting out at midnight or starting at midnight, so you want your guests to be able to enjoy these bonus machines, rather than the team players.

So, since it's a gray area, you must always put the patron first.

62.

Stuffing Coin Chutes, Revisited

There is another way your patrons can be stolen from and not even know it. This is commonly referred to as stuffing coin chutes. A small magnet or small piece of tissue can be put into a coin payout chute. This causes a few coins at the end of a payout to hang up in the chute.

When the patron leaves the machine, the thief just walks up and takes the object out of the coin payout chute, and the snagged coins will fall out. The individual will probably play a coin or two to make sure that his play appears legitimate.

The first indicator of this is rubbernecking, always looking around. The scammer must reach into the coin chute to remove the stuck coin or object.

This type of person will also rarely actually play a machine. They will wander around the casino, bending down, and looking into coin chutes—especially slant tops—and not really spending money in your establishment.

Again, these type of people really stand out, for normal customers are usually enthralled or enjoying the activity they are doing, but this type of person is walking around watching your patrons, looking for every opportunity to relieve them of their money.

A good tell on this is a patron will complain that they are not getting all their coin. The payout chutes of the machines in the area should be checked carefully by slot personnel.

As always, a well trained staff and teamwork between departments prevents this activity. Short pays and blockages should be immediately reported to security and surveillance. An active surveillance department is an effective deterrent to this situation, especially when there is good teamwork with security via radio. A well trained slots staff will immediately report to security any persons attempting to reach into coin chutes.

When these individuals are caught, you notify local law enforcement, according to whatever your particular state laws and regulations are. At the very least, you definitely want this individual removed from your property, and you want all pertinent employees to know what he or she looks like, in case this person comes in again.

63.

Shorting the Players

Another form of internal theft is shorting the players—the employee actually short-changes the customer. Some indicators that this may be occurring are:

1. Unauthorized numerous countdowns of the bank.

2. Hand movement to the body or pockets without clearing them for the cameras.

3. Customer complaints of short rolls: They bought a $10 roll and there was $9.50 in it. This type of activity should be investigated thoroughly.

Shorting the Players: Prevention

1. Good camera coverage over the change machine will show whether all the coins have been emptied out of the bucket or the rack that the patron has turned in to the cashier. Also, see if there are actually coins left in the coin counter or set aside in the tray somewhere.

2. Supervisors should report complaints from guests concerning shortages right away, so surveillance can review the video.

3. Prohibit unauthorized count-downs of the banks.

4. Have the cashier or change person always turn the bucket upside down, showing it to the camera.

5. Tilt the coin-counter tray up into the coin counter freeing all the coins.

The only real way to detect this type of theft is to monitor cashiers and change personnel frequently. Again, a shift manager or above from the slot department can check out videos from the surveillance room and review footage on a random basis.

Investigate thoroughly cashiers or change personnel who have been reported to come up with short rolls, or leave coins in buckets or trays, as previously mentioned. And most of all, always investigate shortage complaints from customers. Money is very personal and the players know how much money they have. Usually the customer is right.

64.

The Short-Change Artist

The short-change artist is in every business wherever money is handled. The basis of a short change scam is to attempt to confuse the cashier with more than one transaction at a time or with sleight of hand. For example, in one hand the short-change artist may have five $20 bills with a $10 bill concealed in the other hand. He asks for a $100 bill. When he is given the $100 bill he turns around and immediately turns back around and says, "I'm sorry, you gave me a $10 bill." When the cashier or change person gives the individual the other $90, of course, the bank will be $90 short.

Never let a customer touch the change or the money.

Well trained personnel in this area know to perform and complete every transaction, one at a time. Remember, money is a very personal thing, and you are dealing one-on-one with your customer.

Review all tapes of cashier windows and cages if any shortages are reported. You do not want a suspected theft on an employee record when in fact it was a short-change artist.

65.

The Pickpocket

This crime is many times made possible by distracting the victim to obtain the article or money. Sometimes the pickpocket will be working alone, but more often with a team. He or she will usually have something over one arm, such as a heavy jacket or sweater, so they can conceal a purse or wallet or other item handed off to them while going in the opposite direction.

There are pickpocket teams that actually travel through different states and countries. They follow jewelry conventions and special sporting events and concerts—anywhere there are large crowds, where it is easy to create a distraction.

There is a type of pickpocket that will carry a large empty bag, such as a shopping bag from the area in which they are roaming or a bag from one of the shops on the property. They will simply pick the mark; when possible they will steal the item by distraction. They may even call security on the person that owns the item and then place the item in the bag and continue walking as if nothing had happened. The stolen article is actually in the bag that was previously empty.

These people know exactly where your money or your item is by the way you move, the way your clothes bulge out, the way you walk. Usually the ones carrying the large bags go more for ladies' hanging bags, backpacks, larger wallets, gifts, and similar items.

To aid your surveillance and security departments in detecting possible pickpockets or distract teams on your property, look for individuals walking around the property examining purses or wallets in an unusual manner. Look for a group of individuals—they may be attending a concert at this property, or it may be a mall during a very busy time around Christmas, or a boxing event, or a convention. They are paying more attention to the people walking around than to the event that they are attending.

If you tend to see the same familiar faces around the casino cage or the ATMs, they may be working that area.

Sometimes a team will enter a property and they will all split up and go information gathering. They have a predetermined meeting place where they meet up and discuss their findings and if they come across any easy targets. The people carrying heavy coats or sweaters over their arms are usually very easy to spot, especially in the hot summer months.

Pickpockets love to work as a team by causing confusion or forcing a lot of people—or the target—into a confined area with other people. If a target has a large amount of money in his right rear pants pocket and is on an escalator, part of the team would be in front of him, part would be in the middle, and part would be behind him. The co-conspirators in the front would stop or cause a delay, causing a backup on the escalator. Confusion would ensue—more of a mild controlled panic, with people bumping into the target—and it is at this point that the target is relieved of his money or wallet.

This works really well on stairwells when events are letting out, like boxing events. You have to walk down just six steps at the most, somewhere along the foyer. The pickpockets will cause a commotion and the target is almost surrounded, because there are normally railings on these types of section stairs. The pickpockets will normally get whatever they want at that time.

One thing we have learned about a pickpocket, through watching training videos and attending different seminars, is that they are very persistent—they never give up.

There is an individual we know, Randolf Felix (he gave permission to use his name), who had done some money crimes. He made a statement that really seems to stick, and we think it's a great quote: "Every second is an option."

Section D:
Skilled Gamblers

66.

Card Counting

People who practice card counting are commonly referred to as *card counters*. These players should be called *advantage players*. They have taken the time and the money to analyze the game of blackjack and develop a good basic strategy of play which, when played correctly, gives the players a very slight advantage against the house.

Card counting consists of a player or players utilizing a memory system to keep track of the cards that have been dealt and what cards remain in the deck(s). The basic counting system is composed of a plus/minus or high/low option. By counting the assigned value of the cards that have been dealt out, the advantage player can often determine the value of the cards that remain in the deck.

With this information, combined with good basic strategy, the advantage player will vary the amount of money wagered. If it has been determined by the advantage player that the remaining cards are rich with face cards and aces, they will increase their bets accordingly and spread out the bets. Of course, if the opposite is in effect and the deck is poor—has few tens and aces remaining—he will reduce his bets.

Card values for a basic plus/minus count system are as follows: Tens, faces and aces equal minus one. Sevens, eights, and nines equal zero. Twos, threes, fours, fives, and sixes equal plus one.

If you were to go through a standard fifty two-card deck—using this high/low count, when you are finished with the deck, the total count would be zero. This count is referred to as a balanced count. A balanced count is one with the point-count value of all the cards in the deck having a sum of zero.

An example of an unbalanced count, the *knock-out system*, or the *KO count*. The only difference between the KO count and the high/low count is that sevens are no longer neutral but are counted as a plus one. When you go through a standard deck in the KO system, the sum of the point count values equals plus four, making it an unbalanced count.

This basic count works very easily for a single deck. However, most casino games are now multiple decks, anywhere from two to eight decks of cards. Advantage players run a deck down what is known as a *running count,* the sum of the point values of all the cards to that point in the shoe. Then they must convert to what is called *true count*, the running count divided by the number of decks remaining in the shoe.

For example, you have a six-deck shoe with approximately two decks left in front of the cut card to be dealt; the running count is a plus six; the true count would be plus three, (two decks left, divided into a count of plus six, to give you a count of plus three).

There are many books about card counting on the market: the one that we have found to be the most informative is *Card Counting for the Casino Executive*, by Bill Zender, published by RGE Publishing, Ltd.

67.

Advantage Players

There are three basic indicators that may lead a surveillance room or floor person-nel to believe that someone is an advantage player:

1. The advantage player must use a betting spread.

2. The advantage player will most likely deviate from basic strategy, especially when the count is in a high plus area.

3. An advantage player will only take insurance (if offered) when the deck is rich, in a very high plus count.

Although most of the decisions made when wagering are simply basic strategy plays, the floor person and surveillance department should be looking for a pattern in the changes of a player's strategy. These types of changes are a big warning sign; the average player does not make these types of moves. The average player is consistent in his or her betting patterns, though they will sometimes up their bet, as a "hunch bet."

When a player (or players) is suspected of being a possible advantage player, information should be passed on to a supervisor or the surveillance depart-ment, and surveillance will run the video back to observe the player in question and determine whether or not he or she is, in fact, an advantage player.

Once the information has been turned over to those concerned, through the proper channels, you want to make sure that you do not tag someone as being an advantage player if he or she is not. Although being an advantage player is frowned upon by most corporations within the casino industry, card counting is not cheating unless one is using some type of device to assist in keeping count of the cards.

Just because someone has the ability to count cards does not mean that the player is going to beat the house. There are a lot of bad players out there who move their money but do not play with the basic strategy, and do not have the patience that a good advantage player would have.

If you receive a confirmation that a player or players are advantage players, there are some things that you must immediately report to a supervisor, the director of surveillance, and the casino shift manager: the bet-spread used; how the player has raised his or her bet to the count; and the different playing strategies observed in relation to the count. There are certain plays that a floor person would see as indicators to call surveillance, that someone may be an advantage player. Some common plays with a large wager would be:

1. Aggressive double-down and splits.

2. Standing during bust situations (player has twelve versus dealer three with true count of plus seven; player stands on the twelve).

3. Insurance is taken only when the player has a large wager—only when the count is high plus.

Small-wagers strategy may be an indicator as well, such as passive double-downs or hitting instead of doubling down. (Player hits eleven versus dealer nine or ten, instead of doubling down.) Common plays with a small wager would be hitting on a normal bust situation (in other words, hitting a fifteen versus a dealer ten) and never taking insurance on a small wager—when the count is low or minus.

There are certain strategies an advantage player uses to dictate surrender; such as a player sixteen versus dealer eight, or a sixteen versus dealer ten—but only on a high plus count. The following circumstances would dictate a surrender to an advantage player.

1. Player fourteen versus dealer ace, at a plus three or greater.

2. Player fifteen or sixteen versus dealer ten, at a plus three or greater.

All these indicators will help you identify and confirm the advantage player within your casino.

68.

Shuffle Tracking

The words *shuffle tracking* seem to intimidate a number of people within the surveillance department and the pit. Because of this intimidation factor, sometimes people don't understand it or learn how to utilize it.

From what I have gathered shuffle tracking was discovered by avid advantage players. Imagine yourself sitting in a shoe game when the count is going very high—but there is one problem: just when you are getting ready to increase your wager accordingly, as a smart advantage player would, the cut card appears and the dealer reshuffles. So now you know that the remaining cards behind the cut card (the slug) are full of tens and aces and you cannot play them. Right? Wrong.

It was discovered that if the player was able to watch where that clump of tens and aces went following the shuffle, it was possible to place the cut card in a strategic location—assuming the player got to handle the cut card or at least keep track its location during the deal. When the slug was reached—the pack of high cards—the player was able to take advantage of this information.

The count at this point really does not matter. The deck can be in a very minus situation, but you bet with both guns, knowing what is to follow—that clump of tens and aces. This makes a great cover and camouflage. The camouflage is that you don't seem to be betting with a count. In some cases you can even wager the table maximum right off the top, if this is where the slug of tens and aces is. If you are a known advantage player, or even suspected of being an advantage player, there will be strategy deviations in your play that an educated player would not normally do, so if casino or surveillance personnel are running your play down, and you are utilizing both card counting and shuffle tracking skills, you could possibly be labeled as a moron or hunch better and nobody will pay you any mind.

The results in shuffle tracking are immediate if it is done correctly, although keep in mind a win is not guaranteed. The more decks in play, the better, for it is harder for cards to be randomly dispersed. Deep shoe penetration of the cut card is not essential.

Shuffle tracking is simply identifying locations in a shoe you want to play. The ideal situation would be to cut the slug to the top of the deck for immediate play. That way all your heavy wagers would be at the front (also known as off the top). There is one catch to this art of shuffle tracking, and it is you must practice, practice, and practice. It has been recommended that one acquire at least six decks of cards and practice at home, visually locating deck segments.

A shuffle tracker must also attempt to learn the shuffles where he is playing, as well as finding the ideal dealer. The more perfect the riffle, the easier it is to track the cards. If you can't map it, you can't track it. So, essentially, the dealer with the tightest shuffle would be the easiest to track. The more practice and familiarity you have with the shuffle you are tracking, the easier the slugs can be located. A good advantage player will always do his homework before walking into the shuffle, knowing what that casino's shuffling procedures are for each game.

Section E:
Card Cheating Techniques

Card Cheating Techniques

Now we are going to get into different cheating techniques that can be used with cards whether the game is twenty-one, baccarat, poker, or any card game, but primarily the game of twenty-one. We are going to give a description of the cheating techniques, how to detect them and, we hope, how to prevent them.

69.

Daub

The description of a daub is a technique used to mark cards to gain information to be used against the house. Normally a daub is a substance that is put lightly on a card in various positions to reveal the value of the card, only known by the person who is doing the daubing or the person that is going to play the daub. A variety of substances are used, such as lip-gloss, hair oil, or any combination invented by the dauber. Most daubs show up on cards as a very light shadow or dull spot. A daub is normally carried on the cheater's person, such as behind the ear, on the neck, or in the palm of the hand. However, the concealment areas for the daub substance can be anywhere the imagination can conceive it.

Sometimes a dauber will use a co-conspirator, such as a woman with the daub placed on the nape of her neck underneath her hair. All the dauber needs to do is put hand to the area of the daub and replenish the amount on his fingers. Once the daubing of the deck is complete, the woman departs the premises, and there is absolutely no evidence on the cheater's person.

One must always be aware that the cards could have been previously daubed by another cheat prior to the money person landing at the game.

70.

Daub: Detection and Prevention

The daub can usually be detected by holding the cards in hand under a light source and tilting the cards back and forth, looking for the dull spot previously mentioned. Another way is to walk behind the table when the cards are being played and get to the spot where the overhead lights reflect off the cards; the daub spots do not reflect like the rest of the cards. In other words, there will be a dull spot.

Observe anyone who is watching the deck or other people's cards, or the dealer's hole card, closer than the average player, especially if he is watching the top of the deck. This is an indicator that the deck may somehow be marked.

Be aware of all over-corrections on betting patterns. Be aware of anyone playing with tinted glasses. There are daubs that can only be detected if the player is wearing a certain type of glasses or contact lenses, or ones that would normally blur someone's vision, in order to see the daub. An indicator of that would be a player who has very thick prescription glasses, and takes them off to play. Sometimes a person with poor vision can detect a daub a lot faster and better than someone with good eyes.

Daubers cannot initiate their trade in your casino if the casino promotes good deck protection. Even if the cards are daubed the player cannot use what cannot be seen. Make certain the cheater cannot see the top card. This is why a dauber will normally look for a weak dealer.

When a daub is suspected, frequent deck changes will discourage even the die-hard dauber because it takes a minimum of twenty-five minutes to daub a deck when it is in play.

Don't assume that a deck of cards has not been daubed if a deck appears to be new and the seal unbroken. All you would have to do is take a fine razor blade, cut the plastic and one of the folds at the side of the box, gently pull the deck out, and daub the deck. Then you replace the deck in the case, close that side of the cardboard case with a little dab of glue, and take a hot match and reseal the plastic. Now the top seal has never been broken. It is rarely caught when done in this manner.

71.

Sorts

The next area of what we call "marked cards" are not actually marked at all. They are called *sorts*. When playing cards are manufactured at the plant, each deck is printed on one large sheet—the whole deck including the jokers and the identification cards—and they are cut all at the same time. Basically, sorts are cards that arrive from the factory not cut evenly. These uneven cards can be sorted out and placed into other decks with the same backing on them; the even ones are slightly different in size from the uneven ones. This allows someone to successfully tell the face value of the sorted cards.

In the case of the classic diamond Bicycle Playing Cards, sometimes the diamond pattern at the sides or the tops of the cards is cut just a little bit differently. For example, the top diamond is cut in half, as opposed to one quarter of the diamond cut in other lots of cards. The cards with the diamonds cut in half can be removed in a certain sequence and placed into another deck, and a reader can read the cards without having to mark them. Where is the evidence of marked cards? There is none, as far as an actual substance. Some cards commonly used in poker rooms are so durable they are frequently washed and used over and over (unlike other casino cards that would be used on a game such as blackjack). Poker cards normally have a border wide enough to find different lots with a smaller or larger border. Once sorted out these cards are put into another deck with the same results. There are also blackjack cards which have wide borders.

72.

Sorts: Detection and Prevention

A common way to detect if a sort is being used is, when a new deck is being introduced into a game, to inspect the edges of the cards for any cards that may have a different edge than the rest of the deck. Sometimes, if you take the deck and rapidly fan it, this will enable the uneven cuts to be seen; when you flip the cards by, it moves and jumps. You can attempt to prevent sorts by ensuring that all decks must be checked before being put into a game.

Do not assume that just because cards appear to be fresh from the factory that everything is okay. Never put a deck into a game that has a broken seal, although a seal, as was discussed earlier, is not foolproof either. Any suspicious decks from any card game should be replaced as soon as possible.

Some marked cards occur naturally, by the environment and by normal handling. Some cards are marked on purpose by the people handling the cards, and are commonly known as crimps, bends, or waves. They are slight bends, waves, or crimps put into a playing card by a player. A crimp bends the card downward, a bend or wave bends the cards upward. When done correctly, this will enable a cheater to determine the value of the dealer's hole card, the next card to be dealt off the top of the deck, and other pertinent information that would assist the player in taking advantage of the house, thus increasing the player's percentage.

From a surveillance standpoint, we find it much easier to detect crimps, bends, or waves with a black-and-white camera with a higher resolution, but that is just a personal preference. You need to observe the cards on the layout for any unnatural shape. It seems to be easier to detect the affected cards by stepping back from the table and observing them from a distance. A supervisor or dealer should be able to detect a bend when the deck is squared up by looking at the ends of the cards, studying both the width and length. A deck that has been altered in this manner, or has any other deformity of any type, should be removed from the game immediately.

Sometimes you cannot stop crimps, bends, or waves, especially if you live in a very humid environment in combination with a casino using a card reader to determine dealer blackjacks. One way to prevent them is to riffle the decks before a shuffle: by squaring the deck on the layout, the dealer riffles with both thumbs working in an upward motion. When done correctly, this move should nullify most bends unless they are put in, in an extreme fashion. Usually a person who employs this marking method will not sit down at a table when a dealer is observed to riffle the decks.

A good way to detect crimps, bends, or waves is to watch for any deck being turned in an unnatural manner. Observe dealers for any type of signals to a player, such as pointing to the hand with different fingers extended when asking if the player would like a hit or not. This is possible sign language. Make sure the dealer is holding the deck correctly and that he is not giving an opportunity for an advantage viewpoint to a co-conspirator. Do not allow a dealer to deal with a loose thumb. Protecting the corners will place the thumb on the corner and not on the top of the card. A corner is most likely where a bend or crimp will occur.

73.

Cooler Decks

A cooler deck is conceivably the most threatening cheating move against a casino. Once it is in place, it is likely a casino will lose every hand until the deck is completed. With a single-deck cooler the effects are obviously fewer because of fewer hands dealt. In the case of a double deck, the losses are approximately doubled. When a cooler deck is used in a shoe, the results are extreme.

A cooler is a deck (or decks) of cards that are presorted and arranged so that when the cards are dealt to a specific number of hands, all the hands will be winners if played correctly. A cooler deck can be introduced into a game primarily in two different ways.

The first and most likely is with the use of an inside conspirator: the dealer and the cheater switch decks. The player brings in the prearranged cooler deck and the dealer hands off the house deck, which in turn is given to another coconspirator who normally depart the premises immediately, getting rid of all evidence. The same technique is usually applied to a double deck, and I have even seen where an entire shoe has been switched.

Once the cooler deck is in, the cheater will most likely bet the maximum amount on hands that the cooler calls for. Usually the initial wagers will be sizable but not to the maximum so as not to draw attention to themselves or the ones around them. With the maximum wagers used, the damages can be devastating.

The second method is almost the same as the first, but without the use of an inside conspirator. This method is very difficult, but is known to be done. The switch is usually done when the dealer places the deck on the layout to be cut by the player. Since the introduction of the cut card now used by most casinos, it is virtually impossible.

Most cheaters will attempt a cooler in a casino with substantial limits, but do not count on the move never happening in a casino with lower limits.

A good way to detect a cooler is to take notice if you observe a new or unknown player placing large wagers when the shuffle or cut was not observed. The game supervisor should become very suspicious if this should happen, and should instruct the dealer to reshuffle and notify surveillance for appropriate reviews. On a blackjack game, one indicator of a cooler deck is based on the fact that the presorted deck only works with a specific number of hands being dealt. So either the table must be full, with every player part of the team, or other patrons attempting to play must be run off or otherwise kept from playing. This does not apply on baccarat, as the number of players does not affect the cards dealt.

Keep in mind that if a cooler is suspected, the dealer is most likely to be involved. Usually the dealer will delay verbal notification of large cheques or money in play so that the game supervisor will not call for a reshuffle because the cards are already in play. Once the cooler is in, the cheater(s) will quickly step up the wager amounts. When the game supervisor suspects that the move has been made, he or she should intervene immediately and order the dealer to shuffle up. This may be vexatious to a player, but the ramifications of a cooler could be more devastating. Sometimes the supervisor may remove the suspected cooler deck from the table, being careful not to alter the card positions, for investigation by casino gaming officials, surveillance, or security.

It should never be forgotten that the cheater is most likely working with a team and that some of the team members may be present on the same table and placing smaller wagers. They will also increase their wagers when the cooler is in effect.

Good enforcement of internal controls is a crucial element; this includes verbal notification before any dealing on "money plays." Acknowledgement from a game supervisor to a dealer is just as essential.

The cheater must have new or used uncancelled cards. This leads to the most obvious prevention: good card control will prevent the dealer from receiving the cooler, from the get-go. Keep in mind that the supervisor may be a coconspirator to the cooler deck's usage.

74.

Cheating at Blackjack

There are a few ways to cheat on the blackjack table without collusion of the dealer. One way is to use what is called a *shiner* or *reflector*. This is a shiny, reflective device that is used to reflect the dealer's hole card to assist the cheater in playing the hand. Reflectors have been used in a variety of ways: a ring, watch, sunglasses, money clip, mirror, and a shaved and polished dime super-glued to the bottom of a nail. Obviously, if the player knows what the dealer's hole card is, this gives a slight edge.

A shiner can also be used by the person dealing the cards to reflect the corner index of a card. This technique is usually used by amateur cheats to cheat in stud poker.

To detect a shiner, any object on the table that has the capability of reflection should be suspect. Be aware of consumption-type objects such as beverages cans, bottles, glasses, or cigarette packs. Sometimes the hands that hold these items will have a mirror underneath them. If the shiner is used while the player is holding it, the hands will be held in a concealment position.

The best way to prevent the use of a reflector or shiner is to regulate what objects are allowed to be placed on the layout. Common sense dictates on this one.

75.

Pressing and Pinching

Another popular way for a cheater to cheat a twenty-one game is called pressing and pinching. What this means is that you add money to (press) or reduce (pinch) your original bet after having information on the outcome of the game. In other words, a player, after seeing his or her cards, increases the amount of the wager for a good hand and decreases the amount for a weak hand, by use of distractions or concealments.

There are a number of ways cheaters have successfully performed this cheating technique. The move is usually initiated when the player places his or her cards under the original wager. To pinch a bet, the cheater's extended fingers drag off chips when he or she is returning the hand to the normal position, being very careful to conceal the chips in the palm of the hand. When the wager is pressed, the same hold true: when the cards are placed under the wager, extended fingers will drop or place additional chips on top of the original wager. Another way to press would be to use the cards to cover the original bet momentarily while adding the chips to the stack. The most likely position for this type of cheater to sit would be on third base, to give the cheater time to consider the cards and to initiate the move while the dealer is busy accommodating the other players. This type of cheat likes to play at a table where the dealer turns his or her body to accommodate the first base, taking third base out of the dealer's peripheral vision. Pinchers and pressers will not use this technique on every hand played, but instead will wait for the most opportune moments. It is more profitable, but much harder to alter the wager from the bottom of the stack.

A good dealer will never let these moves happen. The dealer must be alert at all times and never allow attention to be diverted to any one particular area at a time. The players should never be allowed to come into contact with their money after the cards have been dealt. Never let players pick up their chips and place them on their cards or place the cards on top of the chips.

Pay particular attention to individuals who appear to have a friendship with the dealer, especially ones who are suspected to be dealers in other establishments.

76.

Card Switching

Card switching amongst players to better their hand is very popular. Card switching is usually worked by teams of two or more, though it can be done by one player playing two hands. These individuals are very fast with sleight-of-hand movements.

The team members occupy most of the seats at the table and sit very close together. Usually one person will be placing the larger wager. This is the player who will be assisted in creating the better hand. Both hands of all team members will usually be touching the felt and there will be a lot of commotion on the table with cigarettes, coffee, ashtrays, drinks, and cocktail servers, etc. When the opportunity presents itself a diversion will be created by a team member on the opposite end of the table, diverting the dealer's attention while the card switch is taking place. Often there is another member of the team distracting the pit and floor people into conversation on the other side of the pit. These types of cheaters like to work very busy casinos with a lot of activity and natural distractions. Often the player on one end will completely divert the attention of the dealer, who turns his back to the other end of the table.

To prevent card switching, the cards should be dealt in front of any player's second hand, and the player should not be allowed to touch these cards until the play on the first hand has been completed. If there appears to be an unusual amount of distractions and activity on a game, take notice and have a camera placed on a game. Remember, videotape does not blink and is there for the reason of review.

77.

Bubble Peeking or Heeling

A popular move performed by a dealer to assist an outside player or co-conspirator is known as *bubble peeking* or *heeling*. A capable dealer is able to take a look (a peek) at the top card before it is dealt to gain an advantage for himself or an outside agent. Sometimes a peek is used, resulting in the dealer dealing seconds. More often, once the dealer knows what the next card will be, this information will be passed on to the player, which is obviously to the player's benefit.

There are two common methods, one being the bubble peek and the other heeling. A dealer bubble peeks by sliding the card sideways and pinching the card slightly, causing the corner of the card to arch out and allowing the dealer to view the card within the arch. Heel peeking, or heeling, is when the dealer turns the deck upside down while performing normal actions, such as picking up chips and discards. He slides the top card, enabling the dealer or player to read the top card from the bottom of the deck.

A good way to detect bubble peeking or heeling is to watch for the dealer holding the deck in an unusual fashion. The dealer will have to adjust the view in order to see the cards, such as adjusting eyeglasses with the deck hand or going out of the way so that the player can see the card. A lot of times the peek occurs while the dealer is collecting discards. The discards being held in the opposite hand will cover the deck while the peek occurs. The peek may also occur while the dealer buries his or her hole card while steadying the top card with the opposite hand.

78.

Dealing Seconds

Since we mentioned dealing seconds, let's talk about dealing seconds. This move consists of the dealer having the ability to deal the second card. This move consists of the dealer sliding the top card slightly off the deck, catching the second card with the thumb and bringing it forward and out as in normal dealing.

A good seconds dealer is extremely difficult to detect, unless you know which indicators to look for. It is often believed that dealers deal seconds with a dead thumb; this is not necessarily true. A good seconds dealer will deal seconds with an active thumb, although the indicator of a dead thumb should not be overlooked.

When dealers are going to deal seconds, they must alter their dealing style, which in itself is an indicator that something may be wrong. The dealers actually have to change their learned motor skills and have to give it thought. On a legitimate deal, on the top card, the hand holding the deck will feed the card in a sideways motion to the thumb and forefingers of the hitting hand, resulting in the card coming off with a flip motion. When dealing a second, the dealer must first bring the top card back with the thumb and then grasp the second card and drag it out from the deck to deliver the card.

There is not always a change of rythym in which the cards are dealt. From a surveillance point of view, it appears that the dealer is dealing off the top of the deck.

Sometimes the cards will actually make a noise from the friction of the card being dragged out between the first and third cards.

79.

Dealing Seconds: Detection and Prevention

Look for indications of an unusual move, or anything out of the ordinary:

1. Look for things that Just Don't Look Right (JDLR).

2. Look for any alteration of dealing style or house dealing procedures and policies.

3. Pay particular attention to dealer's thumb on the deck hand. (Notice the thumb on the deck hand to see if it is moving the top card sideways to feed the hitting hand.)

4. Watch for the dealer bringing the deck up to meet his free hand when normally a deck hand would be held stationary.

5. Many times a seconds dealer will actually do the distraction on the game himself to try to divert noninvolved players' attention to anything but the hit card.

80.

Hole Card Play

Earlier we mentioned how a cheater can catch the dealer's hole card by using a shiner, but there are other ways to catch the hole card. It may not even be by means of cheating: it could be a weak dealer and the poor handling of the cards.

Primarily, catching the hole card consists of a player (either a cheater or a recreational player) catching a look at the dealer's hole card. Knowing a dealer's hole card drastically changes the win/loss percentage.

There are a few ways to detect someone who may be catching the hole card. The player will usually sit at the center of the table or in the last seat, sitting very low in the chair. If the dealer is not an experienced one or is just plain sloppy, catching the hole card may not be that difficult to do. When a weak dealer is spotted by a person who wants to take advantage of the situation, that person may return with a co-conspirator who would sit in the first or second seat. The accomplice is normally the money person, while the other person reads the hole card and covertly passes the hole card information on to the accomplice. At this point it would be considered cheating.

81.

Hole Card Play: Detection and Prevention

The game supervisor should monitor a person's play closely if suspicion arises, to determine if the player is staying or hitting correctly during his or her play. A person with knowledge of the dealer's hole card will make unusual hit/stand decisions. Supervisors may also want to have someone stand behind the suspected player to see if the hole card value is visible at any time.

Surveillance cameras may be able to pick up a shadow on the table surface. Sometimes, with a certain type of card reader on the table which requires the dealer to press on the card to push the cards into the reader, the corner of the card can be raised slightly.

The first and most important means of preventing players from catching the hole cards is to ensure that the dealers bury the hole card properly. Proper hole card protection should be strictly enforced, as well as ordered within the internal controls and dealing procedures. Floor personnel should monitor play as well as surveillance to determine if someone is hitting or standing correctly. Observe the individuals at the table and see if any accomplices may be signaling; hand signaling, the slightest movement, or a breath of air may be a signal. This is very hard to detect.

82.

A Sub

A sub could be any place on a dealer's person to conceal chips that have been stolen by the dealer off the game, whether it be craps, Caribbean stud, or blackjack. A sub could be a pocket sewn in the front of the pants or skirt, a French cuff, under a wig, behind a collar or a watchband, behind a tie, etc. What a sub primarily does is transport chips that have been stolen from the dealer into the area where the chip will be concealed until it is converted to cash, when the dealer is off duty or on a break.

A good way to detect the use of a sub is to closely observe a dealer who goes to his body, clothing or hair without clearing or brushing off his hands in the appropriate manner. Sometimes a dealer utilizing a sub will glance around in search of the supervisor's location—in other words, rubbernecking.

If an audit is done on the tables, you will notice that the rack is consistently short whenever a certain dealer is present at that station or bank. A dealer with known bad habits who must supplement his income bears watching. Any dealer leaving the property or building or going to his vehicle bears watching. Beware of the dealer who consistently meets with the same person or persons on break, as this would be a good time for stolen chips to be passed off.

I would say the most effective deterrent would be within the internal controls: forbidding any dealer or games employee from going to their body or clothing at any time while at a game. If they are not allowed to touch themselves, it makes it very difficult to steal, unless they are handing off, but that is a different subject. A good dress code should also be a written policy. Make sure the dealers brush off properly, clear their hands properly, showing the cameras and supervisors open palms prior to going to their body.

A dealer on a dead game should never be reaching into the rack for any reason. This should also be covered in the internal controls.

83.

Mucking

Hand mucking occurs when an individual playing at a card game has a hidden card on his person that he has already taken from the game or brought with him, with the intention of putting that card into play at the opportune time.

Some time during the play the card will be palmed; when the opportunity presents itself, a large wager will come out and the mucker will switch the house card with the palm and turn over a winning hand. At the opportune time the person will make a crossover motion from right to left, placing the ace next to the ten-value card (on blackjack), while simultaneously withdrawing the house card, concealing it in the palm. As a deception, all eyes will be on the left hand as the blackjack is revealed. Of course, after the switch has been made, the person will remove the off card from the table, sometimes placing the card in the pocket or handing the card off to a co-conspirator who walks out with the evidence. This, of course, would not be profitable on a low-limit game. It would be taking an awfully big chance with laws.

Mucking would be more beneficial on a game such as poker than on twenty-one because one can sit there and stay in the game.

84.

Mucking:
Detection and Prevention

It has been our experience that hand muckers like to practice within the casino where they plan to make the move, unnoticed, making small wagers and taking note of the dealers and floor supervisors' awareness: Is the pit trained? What are they watching? Are the dealers looking to get off for their breaks? Is the dealer inattentive or is the supervisor inattentive? The person will simply play, doing nothing wrong, but testing by making false moves on a hand in mucker fashion to see what reaction it may bring. He will be practicing a move with the cupped palms but without a card.

When a person finds that they can make these physical moves without much warning going off to the floor personnel, they will plan their move. If the casino does not react, the mucker knows that this casino is a good target. The person may or may not use a conspirator as a distractor or lay-off person.

Obviously it is much easier at a game where you can handle the cards, but the switch can be done when both cards are on the table by a simple palm move, picking one card up and dropping the other at the same time.

The best way to prevent mucking is to have knowledge of the moves and awareness of the indicators. Muckers give off signals or indicators, which give casino personnel time to stop the move.

The casino should never let a player pick up cards in a concealing fashion. If this is observed, the floor supervisor should be notified immediately and strongly request that the player stop doing this. If surveillance notices an individual doing this, they must make the call to the shift manager or the applicable chain of command for your property. If no intervention is initiated, the mucker will know that the house is a target and will most likely attempt to make the move at a later time. Stopping it at the practice stage will put the mucker on notice.

Here is another signal to watch for: Before the mucker can put a mucked card into play, he or she must first get the card into the hand and onto the layout. Watch for a player making frequent moves to pockets or clothing.

If the use of the mucked card is suspected, suggest that deck be brought down immediately, to ascertain that the correct amount of cards and all of the correct cards are still in play.

85.

The Chip Cup

There is a cheating technique used by a dealer and an outside agent known as a chip cup. I have also heard it called a *Vegas cup*. A chip cup is a cheating device manufactured to the finest precision standards to look like a stack of chips. It is made to act as a person's means of transporting chips out of the dealer's tray and into the hands of a conspirator. The outside of the chip cup appears to be a stack of four chips of a small—usually a five-dollar—denomination. The inside of the cup is a hollow cylinder that has the ability to hold other, higher-value chips so that they can be passed off. In other words, you are hiding higher-denomination chips in a manufactured cylinder painted to look like a stack of lower-denomination chips, such as fives.

When a real chip is played on top of this stack, just offset a bit, the stack looks very good. It is very hard to detect even by surveillance, because they can zoom in on it and it looks exactly like a stack of chips.

So how do you detect it? A player will bet the chip cup with, usually, one real chip on top to bring the device into the game. If he wins the bet, he is paid a normal fashion. However, when a bet is lost the accomplice dealer will bring the cup into the tray and load three chips of a higher value into the cup. Soon there will be a color-change transaction between the player and the dealer; at this point the dealer will pass the cup back to the coconspirator loaded with higher value chips. The outside agent (the player) empties the cup, and the process starts over again.

This is very hard to detect when the move is done with a very good chip cup and the proper technique is used. For the average floor person walking by, or watching from the eye, the cup is almost impossible to detect because of its fine workmanship.

The surest way of detection would be to have a floor supervisor on the alert and a well trained surveillance team that has kept track of the bankroll on the game. If one-hundred-dollar (or higher) chips are missing from the bankroll and cannot be accounted for by studying the player rating cards, then you may have stumbled onto a chip cup. Variances between the table card (which lists amounts of chips going out) and the actual count on the rack are a key indicator of theft, which may be accomplished with the use of a cup. We could try to prevent the use of chip cups, but due to the beauty and simplicity of the chip cup and the fact that it incorporates an employee, it is very hard to prevent. The move requires three certain entities: a dealer, an outside conspirator, and the device itself. If the supervisor were involved, he or she would turn in false ratings to account for the chips taken.

The best defense for a chip cup is a highly trained surveillance department who account for bankrolls. If surveillance has the tools and equipment to track the high-value chips and the win/loss of certain players on the games, the scam will be detected. A well trained surveillance department will use whatever tools are necessary within the rating system of the casino's computer system.

86.

Protecting Your Poker Room

There are things you need to know in order to properly protect a poker room. We will break it down into two areas: cheating from the inside and cheating from the outside.

Cheating From the Inside

Cheating from the inside means from within the personnel of the poker room, such as the dealer, floor person, brush person, etc.

There are many different ways of cheating from the inside:

1. Working with an outside agent setting up hands from discards. In order for this to be successful, a dealer must false shuffle as well as false cut.

2. Giving improper change to a player acting as a co-conspirator.

3. Miscall hands to accommodate a co-conspirator or player.

4. Wearing subs on a dealer's person to conceal chips.

5. Palming paper money during buy-ins from customers.

6. Employees of the poker room, such as shills, working along with dealers by signing out their shill money and tipping it out to their friends to be split up later.

7. Dealing seconds or bottoms. Of course, this would take a highly skilled dealer.

8. Bringing in a cooler deck. This could be devastating, especially during the bad-beat-type poker jackpots that are now popular throughout the country.

9. Overraking the pot to steal later. When the pot is overraked, the moneys go into the table tray. The table bank should always be even, for it is only used to exchange chips for cash. When a pot is overraked and the money put into the table tray, the tray is "over." Example: If you start with a three-hundred-dollar rack and you overrake ten dollars and put the money in the tray, you now have three-hundred-ten dollars and you have to get the ten dollars off the table to a coconspirator, or another employee within the poker room.

10. Dealer bubble peeking at a card to tell a player to stay in or fold.

11. Snatching from the pot, a technique used to extract money from the pot into the palm of the hand while pushing it off to the winning player.

12. Improper change conversion from the pot by the dealer. Example: Dealer takes a dollar of quarters out of the pot and puts it into the table tray, takes a dollar check and puts it into the pot and then removes another four quarters into the table tray. This puts the tray over one dollar and of course shorts the pot one dollar.

13. Intentionally killing hands, concealing their true value from a player who doesn't realize he or she has the winning hand, to accommodate another player on the table.

14. Hiding coin in wrappers. Most poker tables use quarters for change as well as the rake. The quarters usually come in ten-dollar rolls; you will see dealers opening the rolls and putting the quarters into the rack. If the dealer were to leave one or two of the quarters in the wrapper and throw the wrapper away to retrieve it later, the dealer could actually make up to a dollar a roll every time he or she broke for change, which is often.

It would be necessary to make the table bank even, since monies have been removed by committing another theft.

Cheating From the Outside

Cheating conducted by the players:

1. Stealing chips from the pot.

2. Mucking cards in and out of the game: you need to watch for player's hands going on and off the table.

3. Hand signals or any other type of signals to other players to possibly reference the value of a hand or hands.

4. Sandwiching: Putting one player between two others in a series of raises and folds to puff up the betting pattern of the victim.

5. Marking the cards: one of the oldest types of cheating at poker.

Section F:
Casino Games—
Things You Need to Know

87.

Casino Style Poker

Poker is popular throughout the world. It has been proven to be America's most popular card game. According to a variety of authorities, poker contains a greater element of skill than bridge, spades, canasta, or any other card game.

Poker is played with a standard deck of playing cards, consisting of fifty-two cards divided into four suits, clubs, diamonds, hearts, and spades. Each suit has thirteen cards, ranking the ace, king, and queen the highest and the two as the lowest. The objective of the basic poker game is to have the highest-ranking hand.

In a traditional poker game, a hand consists of five cards, although more than five cards are normally dealt. Bluffing is allowed and is an art within itself.

Most card rooms throughout the country have the same general rules with a few twists here and there, with some changes in state laws and regulations. Usually every card room will have written rules that cover the games, as well as internal rules and regulations. The rules should be posted for the patrons to view, or at least in a pamphlet form for you to read. Never, ever participate in a poker game without understanding the rules.

Now we are going to do the ranking order of poker hands: First we will assume there are no wild cards to give a player five of a kind, or any strange rule of an off-the-wall card game. Most of those types of games will not be played in a casino. So we will go with the traditional ranking order of poker hands, in a seven-card or five-card stud type game:

1. The highest-ranking hand is a royal flush: this consists of a ten, jack, queen, king, and an ace, all of the same suite. Example: ten, jack, queen, king, ace (all hearts).

2. The second highest hand is a straight flush: any sequential order of cards of the same suite. Example: two, three, four, five, six (all diamonds)

3. Third is four of a kind: Four of the same value card, in other words, four fours, four sixes, etc.

4. Full House: this hand consists of three of a kind plus a pair. Example: ten, ten, ten, six, and six.

5. Flush: this consists of all cards in the same suite not in order.

6. Straight: any five cards in sequence. Example: two, three, four, five, and six, or seven, eight, nine, ten, and jack. Keep in mind that you need a five or a ten to make any possible straight.

7. Three of a kind: Three cards of the same value: three sevens, three eights, etc.

8. Two pairs: two sets of two cards of the same value. Example: eight, eight, nine, nine, and three.

9. One pair: this consists of any two cards of the same value. Example: five, five, ace, seven, and three.

10. The lowest ranking hand would be a high card such as a king or an ace or any card in your hand that beats your opponent.

All rankings are at face value. The ace is the highest ranking card in games such as stud and Texas hold'em and the lowest ranking card in low-ball games. Full house hands rank according to the value of the card of which there are three of a kind.

To give you an example of the odds of actually getting a royal flush, say, in a five-card poker hand, there would obviously be four possible ways, with the clubs, diamonds, hearts, and spades: the odds in a basic fifty-two-card deck are 649,740 to 1.

88.

Mini-Baccarat

This is the game that the famous British agent 007, James Bond, loves. Baccarat is a casino game that has been around for a very long time. Back in the older days, baccarat was the elite game. All the personnel had formal wear. The men wore tuxedos and women wore evening gowns. Cash was used, not chips. Only the crispest of bills were used.

Now the game has been simplified. Most casinos around the world today will deal the traditional baccarat game, but more and more prefer the mini-baccarat game. So what we are going to do is cover mini-baccarat.

Keep in mind there are house rules, state regulations, and laws that change certain rules and procedures of baccarat as you travel across the country and around the world. These are the basic rules; they can be changed in other areas.

Baccarat is a casino card game that is dealt from either a six- or eight-deck shoe. Two hands are dealt by a house dealer, one to the player hand and one to the banker hand. Before the hands are dealt the wagers must be made. There are three choices to wager on: player, banker, and or tie.

Winning bets on the banker or player are paid even money. If there is a tie, the wagers on the banker and player are returned.

Once a bet has been placed and the first card is out of the shoe, there is no avenue for a change of decision. The bets must stand.

The value of a hand is determined by totaling the value of its cards. Tens and face cards are valued at zero. The remaining cards are counted at face value. Only the last digits of the totals of the cards are used. Example: Player has a six and an eight; the value of the hand is four, because six plus eight equals fourteen, and only the last digit of the total is used. Example: Player has a king and a four, the value of the hand is four. Tens and face cards are valued at zero, the value is four.

The hand with the higher value wins. If both the player and the banker hands are the same total, the bets are returned and all tie bets are paid. A tie bet pays eight to one, but this can differ from casino to casino. The house makes its money by a commission, also known as vigorish or vig, normally five percent, which is charged by the house on all winning bank bets. Some casinos have been known to change their commissions and fluctuate with the players' needs.

The main object of the game is to wager on which hand will total closest to the number nine.

The Game

After the bets are placed, the dealer pulls four cards from the shoe. First and third are the player's hand and second and fourth are banker's hand.

Player Hand Rules: Once the player and banker hands first two cards each are dealt, the player hand must stand or draw according to the following rules: If the player's first two cards total six or more, the player must stand and may not draw a card. If the player's first two cards total five or less, the player must draw one card.

There is also what is called a natural. A natural is when the hand total is eight or nine within the first two cards dealt. This applies to both the player and the banker hand, and it wins automatically, except against another natural of greater or equal value. If one hand has a natural, the other cannot draw, but loses immediately, unless it ties or wins with another natural eight or nine.

Banker Hand Rules: These rules are used throughout the world, but may differ slightly if the banker's first two cards total seven or more, the banker must stand and cannot draw a card. If the banker's first two cards total zero, one, or two, the banker must draw one card. If the banker's first two cards total three, four, five, or six, the banker may or may not draw a card, determined by whether the player drew a card as well as the value of the player's draw card.

89.

Roulette

Roulette is an exciting game for a player because of its visual action, and it is a pure game of chance. A wheel goes round and round, a little white ball is spun, and the ball hits these shiny objects and makes noise and clinks and dings, and there are different colors on the table and different colored chips, and the excitement is sometimes overwhelming.

There is no skill needed to play the game and no known legal way to reduce the house advantage. Tracking the wheel looking for certain hot spots or numbers to hit more than others takes thousands of spins. It could work if you had the time and had pinpointed a biased wheel. Is that information available to the public? Yes.

Roulette has been traced back to seventeenth-century France. The wheel contained no zero and paid true odds. The American wheel with a single zero and a double zero has a house advantage of approximately 5.26 percent. The game is not as popular in the States as it is in Europe, because in Europe they did not have the double zero, actually reducing the house advantage down to about 2.8 percent. However, most casinos even in Europe now use the double-zero-wheel.

In roulette each spin is a new spin, and the outcome is not dependent on previous spins. The probability of any certain outcome is exactly the same for each spin. Believe it or not, that little white ball does not care where it lands. The ball does not know where it landed before, and it does not know where it will land next. The ball does not even know it's a ball.

If you believe that you may have a biased wheel, do a wheel audit. It could be caused by a number of factors, such as wear and tear, manufacturing defect, etc. Try switching to a larger roulette ball or a smaller one. Some casinos switch balls every three or four spins or even every other spin.

There are no true systems that work other than luck. A system player is exactly what the casinos want. The player may win once in a while, but eventually the house advantage will overcome. This is mostly because a system player tends to spend long hours playing more than and longer than the average player.

If the players really want to keep track of the spins, by all means give them the means to do it: we have the track and display board.

Have you seen the ads in the paper that tell you for $19.95 you can purchase sure-fire roulette systems? Well, don't waste your money. Do you really think that anybody who could win at roulette would be bothering with a newspaper ad rather than traveling around the world making millions?

The game of roulette is based on a random selection of one number out of a selection of 38. The layout is designed to allow the player a combination of many different wagers for each spin of the ball. The wheel should have a perfectly balanced center. It is rotated manually in a counter-clockwise direction; the ball is spun in a clockwise direction. The pockets in which the ball lands are of equal size, and the partitions between each number are of equal height. Due to all of the different obstacles and the fact of opposite rotation of the ball and the wheel, a random selection is almost assured.

This of course assumes that the wheel does not have any "hot" numbers caused by wear or defects, or any type of predictability, or of course any type of cheating.

Players who buy into the game are issued nondenominational chips with which to play. Each player is assigned and issued a different color; his or her chips are valued at the table minimum, or are marked for a higher value. When a player is ready to leave the game, the dealer will normally cash out the chips for regular casino value chips, to be cashed in at the cage or for play at another game.

You must know the roulette payoffs to properly protect the game:

1. Straight-up bet: chip(s) placed on a single number: pays thirty-five to one.

2. Split bet: chip(s) placed on the line between two numbers; pays seventeen to one.

3. Street bet: chip(s) placed on three numbers (such as four-five-six); pays eleven to one.

4. Corner bet: chip(s) placed on a corner between four numbers; pays eight to one.

5. Top line bet: chip(s) placed on the top line next to the one and single zero, covers zero-double zero-one-two-three; pays six to one.

6. Double-street bet: chip(s) placed on a line covering six numbers (such as four-five-six-seven-eight-nine); pays five to one.

7. Pocket bet: there are three pocket bets, zero-double zero-two, zero-one-two, double zero-two-three; pays eleven to one.

8. Column bet: covers any one of three columns one the layout, twelve numbers; pays two to one, loses on either zero.

9. Dozens bet: covers the first, second or third twelve numbers; pays two to one, loses on either zero.

10. Black or red: covers eighteen numbers, corresponding to the colors on the layout; pays even money, loses on either zero.

11. Even or odd: covers the eighteen even odd numbers; pays even money, loses on either zero.

12. Top or bottom: covers the first or last eighteen numbers; pays even money, loses on either zero.

These are the other roulette terms you need to know:

1. Bowl: the part of the roulette table that houses the wheel.

2. Canoe: refers to objects placed on the sides of the wheel that break the drop of the ball when it falls. They increase the randomness of the game.

3. Double zero: the thirty-eighth number on a roulette wheel.

4. Green: refers to the zero and double zero.

5. Frets: the partitions which separate the number pockets on the roulette wheel.

6. Neighbors: refers to the numbers adjoining the winning number on the wheel itself.

7. Inside: includes all bets placed on less than twelve numbers.

8. Outside: all betting areas outside the numbers. Includes all two-to-one and even-money bets, placed on twelve or eighteen numbers.

90.

Let It Ride

Let It Ride is a casino game that was created in 1993, and it is simply a variation of five-card poker.

Keep in mind that rules do change from state to state, from gaming enforcement division to gaming enforcement division. The table on which Let It Ride is dealt resembles that of a blackjack table, but with different types of markings on the felt. The house dealer distributes the cards to the players; there are seven player positions, each with three designated betting spots. Before the cards are dealt the players must place three equal value wagers in each betting circle. Most casinos have adopted a five-dollar minimum, but this can be raised or lowered by the house.

What makes this game fun and interesting is that the player has options and strategy decisions to make, accompanied by a lot of lights, bells and whistles, music, cocktails, fun, dance, and of course song.

How to play: A standard deck of fifty-two cards is used; no jokers. Most houses prefer poker-sized cards. The players make their wagers of three bets of equal amount. After all the bets are down, the dealer delivers three cards face down to each player.

The dealer receives two cards face down. The two cards the dealer has are community cards, just like in the game of hold 'em. After the players review their hands, but before the dealer reveals the first community card, the players have the option of removing the first of the three wagers.

The dealer turns up one of the two down cards, and the players may elect to have the second wager removed or to leave it. Players tuck their cards under the final bet. Once the second option is completed, the dealer turns up the second card.

The players now make the best hand possible using their three cards and the two community cards the dealer has turned over. Players are paid on the remaining wagers and according to a set schedule normally used through out the industry. Payoffs vary according to house rules; there are also some games with bonuses for very high hands.

91.

Caribbean Stud Poker

Caribbean stud is truly a casino table game. It is played on a modified twenty-one table and is based on the standard five-card stud poker game. It is also the first casino table game to offer a progressive jackpot.

Each player makes an opening wager or ante; players also have the option to bet one dollar to participate in the progressive jackpot. By participating in the progressive jackpot, players have the chance to win all or part of the progressive jackpot with a royal flush; straight flush, four of a kind, full house, or flush.

After the progressive jackpot wager decision is made and the cards have been dealt, players then have the option to bet to call the dealer. If the players feel their hand can beat the dealer, a wager will be made that is twice the amount of the ante bet. If the players feel their hand cannot beat the dealer, the hand can be folded and the ante is lost to the house.

The dealer must have a hand of an ace and king or higher to continue. (This qualifying hand for the dealer may vary according to local rules.) If the dealer does not have an ace-king or higher, the hand is over, and the dealer will pick up all the cards and pay off only the ante bets to those players still in the hand.

If the dealers hand is ace-king or higher, then the players must beat the dealers or lose their bets. The winning wagers are paid, along with any additional bonus money if applicable.

The Rules of Caribbean Stud

1. The player must place a wager. This is also called an ante.

2. Each player and the dealer is dealt his or her own five-card hand. One of the dealer's cards is face up; the other four are face down.

3. The player must decide to stay in or fold. Folding forfeits the player's ante. To stay in, the player must make a second bet equal to his or her ante.

4. The dealer looks at his or her cards. If the dealer does not have at least an ace and king, then the player automatically wins even money on the ante and the additional wager is returned. If the dealer does qualify with an ace-king, a comparison is made between the player's hand and the dealer's hand. If

the player has the higher hand the player is paid even money on the ante and the additional wager is paid according to the payout scale on the table. If the dealer can stay in with at least an ace-king, and the player does not have the higher hand, then the player loses both the ante and the additional wager.

Payoffs on winning hands are made according to a schedule which is printed on the layout. Payoff amounts can differ from area to area. The problem with Caribbean stud from the player's point of view is the requirement that the dealer have an ace-king minimum. It is not odd for a player to have a very strong hand and have the dealer not qualify on that hand. Consequently, the player gets paid even money on the ante and the additional wager is returned. However, bonus payoffs from flush up to royal flush are not subject to dealer qualifying, or even winning. As long as the player had made the bonus wager, he is paid his portion of the bonus for any qualifying hand.

92.

Pai Gow Poker

Pai gow poker is an interesting and fun game for the casino gambler. The game offers a combination of dice, cards, and poker.

The game is played with a standard deck of fifty-two cards plus a single joker. The joker can be used only as an ace or to assist in making a straight or a flush. A cup containing three dice is shaken and the results of the roll determine the position of the first hand to be dealt, starting from the banker's hand. The banker's hand is always considered number one. Example: The banker (in this case the dealer) will always receive the first hand when the dice total eight or fifteen.

In front of each player are two marked areas, one marked high hand and the other second highest. Each player and the dealer are dealt seven cards. The object is to use the seven cards and divide them into a high hand of five cards and a low hand of two cards. Stud poker rules are used; the only difference is that in pai gow poker the player needs to beat both the banker's high and low hands to win. Example: The player beats the banker with one hand and the banker beats the player with the other hand: it's a tie. The bet is returned. Each player is offered the opportunity, in turn, to act as a banker. This rule, as well as any rule, can change from house to house. In pai gow poker, if acting as banker, the player banks against the house as well as the other players at the table. If a player is going to act as a banker, the player must have the bankroll to pay off all the wagers should the banker lose. The house makes its money by charging a five percent commission on all winning bets, as in baccarat. One other rule that is in favor of the house is that if a player's high or low hand is identical to the dealer's, the dealer wins on the identical hand.

93.

Craps or Dice

In craps the player throws a pair of dice and wagers on the result of each throw. Additional players may make the same or different wagers on the same rolls of the dice.

There are many different types of bets to choose from, with different win or lose conditions. These bets can be placed by the players at different times as the game progresses.

There are basically two dice rolls: the come-out roll and the point roll, which is any roll of the dice after a "point" is set, and before that point is rolled again, or a seven is rolled.

The come-out roll is always the first roll in an attempt to establish a point. A point is established when a four, five, six, eight, nine, or ten is rolled; the player must roll that number again in order to "make his point," before rolling a seven.

Bets:

Pass Line: If a two, three, or twelve is rolled on the come-out roll, the pass line wagers lose. If a seven or eleven is rolled on the come-out roll, the pass-line wins. If the come-out roll is a four, five, six, eight, nine or ten, that number becomes the point.

Don't pass: opposite of betting pass line. The wager loses if the come-out roll is a seven or eleven and wins if a two or three is rolled. The number twelve is no-win, no-lose situation. If four, five, six, eight, nine, or ten is rolled on the come-out roll, this is the point. If a seven is rolled before the point is rolled, the don't pass wins. The wager loses if the point is rolled before a seven is rolled.

Come bets: The come bets is made anytime after the come-out roll. Wagers win if a seven or eleven is rolled and lose on a craps of two, three, or twelve. Any other number that is rolled becomes the come point and the wager wins if the come point is rolled before a seven. Wagers are moved by the dealers from the come area to the area of the come point and paid if the number rolls again prior to a seven.

Don't come bets: The reverse of a wager on the come. The wager loses on a seven or eleven rolls and wins on a two or three. Again, twelve is a push. The wager wins if a seven is rolled prior to the come point and loses if the point is rolled before a seven is rolled.

Odds: Although there are many different odds bet to deal with in the game of dice, we are going to look at some specific basic ones that you need in order to protect the game.

A player may take odds or lay odds in addition to the original flat bet. Flat bet means the original pass line, come bet, don't pass, or don't come bets. A flat bet is paid even money. The odds are as followed:

Pass Line and Come Bet-Odds

> Four and ten pay two to one
> Five and nine pay three to two
> Six and eight pay six to five

Don't Pass Line and Don't Come Bet-Odds (Lay)

> Four and ten pay one to two
> Five and nine pay two to three
> Six and eight pay five to six

Place bets can be made at any time on any or all of the following numbers: four, five, six, eight, nine, or ten. If the number placed rolls before a seven is rolled, the place bet wins and is paid the following odds;

> Four and ten pay nine to five
> Five and nine pay seven to five
> Six and eight pay seven to six

Proposition bets: All proposition bets are one-roll bets. They win or lose on each roll. Examples: horned bet (two-three-eleven-twelve); crap-eleven; any seven.

Hard Ways: there are only four possible hard ways wagers to be made the pairs two-two, three-three, four-four, five-five. Hard four pays seven to one; hard six pays nine to one; hard eight pays nine to one; hard ten pays seven to one. If any other combination of the number or a seven is rolled, the hard-way bet is a loser. In other words, if you have a bet on the hard ten and a six-four is rolled, your hard way ten bet is a loser. If double fives are rolled, then your hard-ten bet is a winner. If a seven rolls, all hard-way bets lose.

Buy and lay bets may be made at any time on numbers four, five, six, eight, nine and ten. The buy bets win if the number is rolled before a seven. The lay bet wins when a seven is rolled before the number. Usually there is a vigorish collected by the house on a buy or lay bet because these bets pay true odds. A commission, normally 5 percent, is charged on the amount of the payoff.

Field bets: another one-roll bet that can be made on any roll. There are seven numbers within the field area; two, three, four, nine, ten, eleven, and twelve. Normally the numbers two and twelve pay two or three to one; all other numbers pay even money. The amount on the two and twelve varies house to house.

The big six and the big eight: even money wager. The wager may be increased or decreased or taken down anytime between rolls. The bet wins if a six or eight is rolled before a seven.

On a set of dice, there are thirty-six total possible combinations, six from one die times six from the other die. This is what creates the odds on each number. Example: the number four has three possible combinations: a one and a three, a two and a two, and a three and a one.

94.

Dice Protection

There are several ways to detect if the dice have been altered. They can be improperly balanced, misspotted, misshaped, trimmed, or loaded with a foreign substance. The different ways of fixing or "gaffing" the dice can be detected by a few simple tests or other methods of examination that can be performed at the table or in the pit.

One of the first things is to check that each die has the proper number of spots. Starting with the ace side of the die, make sure that all opposing sides of the die when combined total seven. Go through each combination of the die. Example: If the side you are looking at is a three, then the opposite side will be a four.

One of the methods of fixing or altering dice is to misspot certain sides of the dice; this will guarantee that certain numbers will or will not roll. Some of the most common misspots are a pair of dice that have just twos, fours, and sixes on them or a pair of dice that have aces, threes and fives only. Notice that neither of these pairs of dice, when rolled, will roll a seven.

If one of the ace-three-five dice were put into play with one of the deuce-four-six, this would be considered a set of miss-outs. These dice would roll twice as many sevens as a legitimate set of dice.

Keep in mind that some dice are only misspotted on one side, which would make it impossible to roll a certain number.

The best way to test dice is to measure all sides with a micrometer. A micrometer can be bought through any gaming supply catalogue or any game store that deals with equipment related to gaming. Scientific supply and precision tool stores and catalogs also carry them. No matter what size dice your casino uses, all three directions should measure (mike out) to a difference of no more than three ten-thousands of an inch (.0003"). Most dice companies guarantee their dice to within one ten-thousandth of an inch.

When using the micrometer make sure that you check each die in all three directions. It is best to go with a standard pattern such as miking the ace-six side first, followed by the deuce-five, then the three-four, in order, to help you keep track.

Some of the best ways to check dice are done right at the table at the time, which is when you really want to catch bad dice being put on. This would normally be done by the box person. Dice that are intentionally gaffed are usually altered so much that the difference can be picked up with the naked eye by a highly trained staff.

When the dice are brought back to the middle of the table by the stick person, they are first left side by side before they are spread apart. When the dice are together, check and see if the dice appear to be the same height and width. This is why they place the dice in front of the box person first. The variations may only be ten ten-thousands of an inch, but this is enough to alter the outcome of the roll.

By spinning a die you can tell if the die is evenly balanced. This is normally done by spinning the die with a tool known as a caliper. A lot of times you will see box people spinning them in their fingers; this takes a lot of practice but it is possible. I have seen box people with years of experience spin that die between their thumb and their middle finger and have it spinning so fast and long that you would actually think they were actually using a caliper.

When you spin the die, you are primarily looking for loads, which intentionally put the die out of balance, causing them to favor certain numbers. As a result, when loads are spun, they will wobble noticeably. For the best result, it is recommended that the tested die be spun on all three access points. Some loads will react differently in a different direction. They will not noticeably wobble as much.

As primitive as this may sound, it is not a bad idea to check the dice with a magnet or to keep a compass on the table to see if a magnet may be present. A strong enough magnet will affect the roll of a die. You can also place a small magnet over and around a die to ensure that materials have not been inserted into it that will react to a magnetic field.

The best way is to know how to read the dice in any position. To do so, you would have to know the proper spotting of your dice. Some dice are manufactured slightly differently. It is important that you study the dice used in your casino and know the sequence of them, no matter what position they are in. This is to your advantage.

There is also what is known as advantage play in craps. There are many players who are performing techniques known as "control shots." The thrower can kill the number on one die when rolling, which gives him a 1 in 6 chance to make point or a 1 in 3 chance to roll 7 or 11 on the come out roll.

95.

Dice Terminology

Here is the basic dice terminology you need to know for report writing, to properly protect the game, and for communication with people outside your surveillance department.

All the way: To bet all available resources.

Bank craps: When the players bet against the house.

Bevels: Dice that have their edges smoothed or rounded compared to a sharp edge. Can be used with a cheating technique when only some edges are rounded so that certain dice combinations are more likely to be rolled then other numbers.

Bones: Slang for dice.

Bowl: The container in which the three unused dice are kept on the dice table.

Box cars: A pair of sixes in craps.

Box person: The person who sits between the two dealers behind the table. Normally the supervisor.

Bust out person: A dealer or box person who switches the dice on a craps game, or someone who uses a cheating method.

Buy bet: A bet in which a player may purchase the true odds on any number on a crap game but must pay a small percentage to the house, also known as a vig or vigorish.

Come: The place on a craps table to place bets after the point has been established on the pass line, for numbers four, five, six, eight, nine, and ten. This enables a player to bet on the next roll of the dice.

Concave: A die or dice that have one or more sides beveled inward, which assists the die or dice to stop on those sides face up.

Convex: A die or dice that have one or more sides beveled outward, causing the die or dice to roll off these sides.

Craps: A roll of two, three, or twelve on the come-out roll. Pass line loses; don't pass wins on two and three but pushes on twelve.

Cubs: Another slang term for dice.

Dice bowl: Normally made of wood or rubber, it stores the dice that are not being used by the players. A normal number of dice to be put on a game would be five, so three would stay in the bowl and of course two would be utilized at a time.

Ductors: Loaded dice that will only roll two or three numbers.

Don't bet: A bet on the don't pass or don't come line. A bet that the dice will not pass or come, meaning a seven is rolled before that number.

Easy way: Rolling a four, six, eight, or ten with the dice showing different numbers, rather than in pairs as a hard way. Example: one-five or four-two rather than two threes.

Fever: The five point in dice, also known as a phebe.

Flat, or flats: Dice that have been cut down to the point that they are no longer square. This causes the dice to fall off the narrow sides and land on the wide sides.

Floating load: A die with heavy base material inside of it that can change its physical position within the cube.

Hard way: Even numbers that can be made using two dice with the same number on each die.

Hop bet: When the player calls the way the dice will land on the next roll, specifically the particular combination, a two-five or a four-two.

Horned bet: A one-roll proposition bet on two, three, eleven, and twelve.

Hot Streak: A run of good luck.

Ivories: Slang for dice.

Juice: 1) Another name for a commission or vig that a player must pay, for example, in a baccarat game. 2) A connection or someone you know who may be an influential person, or that person's influence.

Laying odds: A bet of a larger amount against a smaller amount.

Layout: The felt on the table on which the game is played which is marked with specific areas for each bet. It enables the dealers to keep track of several wagers at one time.

Loaded dice: Dice that are weighted or otherwise modified to make sure that only certain numbers can be rolled.

Misspots: Dice that do not have all six numbers so that certain numbers or combinations cannot come up.

Natural: The numbers seven or eleven on a come out roll.

Odds bet: Wagers made with pass line and come bets, after these points are established, that pay greater than even money.

Pass line: Area on the layout where players bet on the come-out roll. It wins on seven or eleven on come-out roll, wins on the second roll of the point, and loses on two, three or twelve on come-out roll.

Percentage dice: Dice that have been altered by changing the shape and or edges so that the selected combinations will be rolled more often.

Proposition: Bets on one roll chances.

Puck: The device that is used to mark the point.

Razors: Dice with edges which form a sharp right angle.

Scooting: A cheating technique used while throwing the dice. The dice do not bounce or roll, enabling the preset combination to remain true. This is the same as sliding the dice.

Sitting the box: The crap game supervisor who sits on a chair or stool located between the two dealers who are paying the bets; also referred to as the boxman.

Snake eyes: Two aces on a pair of dice.

Snowballs: Dice that only have fours, fives, and sixes.

Stick: The tool used by the stick person to retrieve and present the dice to the shooter. The stick person uses the stick, runs the crap game, and calls the rolls.

Total: A payoff made on a crap table which includes the original wager and the payoff all in one stack.

Vigorish: A percentage paid by players for buy and lay bets and often hop bets. Also known as vig or juice.

World bet: A five-part proposition bet that includes two, three, seven, eleven, and twelve on a single roll of the dice. Also known as "around the world."

96.

Casino Fill and Credit Slips

Fill Slip

Document used to track and transport monetary instruments to a gaming table.

A fill slip should contain all pertinent data related to the fill amount:

1. Total

2. Game and table number

3. Date and time

4. Breakdown of each denomination

5. Signatures of all parties involved with the fill.

On the average, most fill slips involve four copies:

1. One is dropped into the table game drop box.

2. One in a temporary file, usually within the cage.

3. One returned to the cage with all signatures required.

4. One retained within the machine which originally printed the fill slip.

Credit Slip

Document used for the transport of monetary instruments from a game to the cage. Follow the procedures dictated by the internal controls of your property.

Summary—Games

We've seen the basic rules of many games here. In order to learn these games well, you should attend a class on each one. There are always new games being tried. Learn the rules, procedures, and methods of play.

Section G:
A Look at Indian Gaming

97.

A Look at Indian Gaming

Indian Country is a statutory term that refers to all lands within an Indian reservation, dependant Indian communities, and Indian Trusts.

The number of tribal compacts with the various states where the specific Indian tribe has a casino(s) is less than half of the member of five-hundred-sixty-one tribes recognized by the federal government. There are two-hundred-fifty-five tribal state gaming compacts or covenants in twenty-nine states. Some tribes have more than one casino facility. Tribal gaming revenue is approximately ten billion dollars, and this represents less than 10 percent of the total gaming industry. Tribes operate gaming casinos for more than the money, although that's reason enough. They do it primarily to generate employment for the tribal members, although through personal knowledge we know that many employees, particularly in support functions, are non-Indian. There are over two-hundred thousand jobs in the industry. The percentage of Indians to non-Indians in the workplace is 25 to 75.

The Indian Gaming Management Staff of the Bureau of Indian Affairs Washington, D.C., maintains the listing of tribal-state compacts. What the compacts authorize is the types of gambling and games of chance that are offered at the facility. It includes just about everything: blackjack, money-wheel, roulette, baccarat, chuck-a-luck, pai-gow, chemin de fer, craps, horses, beat the dealer, poker, over-under seven, beat my shake, keno, on line games, lottery tickets, punch boards, pull tabs, slot machines, paddle wheels, acey-deucey, and many others.

Where Does The Money Go?

The Indian Gaming Regulation Act, 25USC 2710 Section 11, requires that tribal gaming revenues can be used for no other purpose than

> Funding tribal government and or programs
> Promoting tribal economic development
> Assisting in funding operators of local government
> Providing for the welfare of the tribal members

Forty-seven tribes that have the approval of the secretary of interior to make per capita payments to tribal members as part of their revenue allocation plan. It is important to note that the tribal members pay federal income tax on these payments.

Who's Watching Whom?

There are three levels of regulations for tribal gaming. The Indian nations are primarily the regulation under the Indian Gaming Regulatory Act (IGRA). The tribes establish the framework and are self-policing. State regulations maybe included in the Compacts between the Tribe and the State. Federal agencies cover the laws relating to Indian gaming. These include the following;

>   National Indian Gaming Commission
>   Interior Department
>   Justice Department
>   Treasury Department
>   Secrete Service
>   FBI
>   IRS
>   Financial Crime Enforcement

Federal law makes it a crime to steal, embezzle or cheat from an Indian gaming operation. It is punishable by up to 10 years in prison under 18 USC, Sec:1163.

A final comment about all the good that Indian Casino Gaming does for assisting through funding operations of local governments. It is enormous. Equipment, substance abuse programs and so much more benefit from Indian generosity.

98.

Regulations and Surveillance in Indian Gaming[18]

With the passing of the Indian Gaming Act in 1998, gaming was opened up to all recognized Indian Nations in states where gaming was allowed. Class I and II gaming were already present on many reservations, but now the chance to incorporate Class III, or "Las Vegas Style" gaming, was available. The act was actually passed because the government felt that they needed a way to regulate the gaming that was already occurring on many reservations across the United States.

Surveillance in Indian casinos is a challenge in many cases. Rumors about Indian casinos being loosely regulated are not true. The first group of regulations that Indian casinos must deal with is the National Indian Gaming Commission (NIGC). This sets the Minimum Internal Control Standards (MICS) for all Indian Casinos. The NIGC regulations are monitored by the NIGC on a regular basis to make sure that all departments are in compliance.

The NIGC applies to surveillance in depth. First the regulations set down the rules for the surveillance room itself. This section covers location of the room and access to the room. Next are the regulations on satellite systems, followed by regulations on power outages and back-up power, the section on time-and-date generators and their requirements. Staffing is next, followed by video monitors and repairs of surveillance equipment. This is followed by regulations on what must be done in case of a malfunction of a dedicated camera. A section is included on what must have dedicated camera coverage, including progressive slot machines and the live games area. The section then breaks down not only what must be covered, but what must be seen through the camera in the coverage. Regulations then move on to general overview cameras and where and what must be covered by those. Next it moves on to videotapes and their retention and tapes that are evidence in active cases. Regulations, then, deal with the numerous logs required and the data that must be kept on each log.

To go into detail on each of the regulation and the overall process would take many pages of material.

---

[18]Premission to reproduce obtained from the author, James Stone.

The state gaming commission regulates the compact between the state and Indian nation. They also enforce state gaming laws and monitor the casinos for violations of compact, NIGC regulations, state law, and gaming regulations. In most states the agents of the state gaming commission are sworn law enforcement officers with the full powers of a law enforcement officer. State agents are usually on property on a daily basis.

After the Indian casino takes all the steps to comply with the state gaming commission, they must also deal with the next step in regulation, the gaming commission of their tribe. The tribal gaming commission is charged with the job of regulating the tribe's own internal control standards, which must be in compliance with NIGC, as well as making sure the casino is in compliance with the state compact, state laws, and state gaming regulations. The employees of the tribal gaming commission are on property 24 and 7, making sure all regulations are followed.

Because of all the regulations, and variations in how surveillance rooms are supervised, many challenges outside of the surveillance operator's duties can be present. With all the different agencies regulating the activities of the casino, there are differences in interpretation of the regulations. This can become troublesome for surveillance personnel, as sometimes it can be a long time before the issue is settled, causing some uncertainty in carrying out their duties. This doesn't happen all that often anymore, as the casinos have been around for several years now, but many casinos still have "growing pains" now and then.

Supervision of the surveillance department varies from tribe to tribe. In some tribes the surveillance department is a part of the tribal gaming commission. Other tribes have the surveillance department reporting to the tribal council, and still others have them report to the management of the casino. The most common is that the surveillance department is a part of the gaming commission.

Probably the biggest shortfall early in the history of Indian casinos was not the equipment, but the training that was received. This is not an issue anymore, as many tribes have been very wise in their training, using the resources available to them to train top-notch staffs.

Many Indian casinos have all the same tools that are present in the Las Vegas casinos. Surveillance systems have become elaborate, and many Indian casinos have kept up with the technology. Using modern resources that allow casinos to stay in contact with each other, facial recognition resources, and other modern technology, Indian casino surveillance rooms are on the cutting edge of technology. However, technology alone will not be effective without a well trained and supervised staff.

Section H: Information to Make Sure That You Are Working With Proper Equipment

99.

Surveillance Room

The surveillance room should be maintained at a level where entrance to the room is not readily accessible by other casino employees who work primarily on the casino floor. Access to the surveillance room should be very limited and be left up to the key management personnel of that property. In most states, any agent or investigator of a state gaming enforcement division has full access at all times.

All monitors and massive controls and key elements of the equipment for the surveillance room are kept within the surveillance room itself. This allows your surveillance personnel to have total override capability of all other satellite types of surveillance equipment located outside the surveillance room.

Your surveillance system must have a time-and-date generator that is able to display the time and date of the recorded events on your videotapes. The time and date stamp should not obstruct any important part of the recorded view.

Every surveillance room should have an auxiliary or back-up power unit. In the event power is lost to the surveillance system, this auxiliary or back-up power unit is immediately available and capable of providing immediate restoration of power. This unit should support all elements of the surveillance system that enable the surveillance personnel to observe the table games remaining open for play and all areas covered by important, high-priority dedicated cameras.

Once you have your surveillance room equipped, you must have surveillance personnel. The surveillance room should be staffed with personnel highly trained in the use of the equipment, knowledge of the games, house rules, procedures, laws and regulations, investigative techniques, etc.

The surveillance room should never be unattended, if at all possible. There are times when, because of sicknesses or shortness of staff during vacation periods, one person may have to manage the surveillance room by immediately activating a cellular-type telephone or other communication device to transfer all calls while the person is using the restroom or taking appropriate meal and room breaks.

Your surveillance personnel must also have the ability to get up and exit the surveillance room and take a walk or get some fresh air. We feel that surveillance personnel should eat separately from casino personnel to maintain distance and anonymity.

100.

Surveillance Cameras

Each camera should be installed in a manner that prevents it from being readily obstructed, tampered with, or disabled. Somewhere in casino internal controls there should be a rule that forbids employees from intentionally obstructing cameras. I think any employee found to be intentionally obstructing a surveillance system should be immediately reported to the appropriate chain of command.

- Cameras are used to observe gaming and gaming related activities and are used in areas of prime concern and vulnerability.

- Fixed cameras are stationed with no ability to pan, tilt, or zoom.

- A dedicated camera is one that continuously records a specific area or activity.

- A motion-activated camera records a specific activity or area upon any detection of activity or motion.

- A pan-tilt-zoom camera (PTZ) is able to pan, tilt and zoom. Normally the PTZs are encased in smoked domes or a type of plexiglass bubble— sometimes behind one-way mirrors—or a similar material that can conceal a camera from view, making it almost impossible to determine when it is in use or where it is pointed.

Each video camera should be able to have its picture displayed on a video monitor as well as having it recorded within the surveillance room. A properly equipped surveillance room will have a sufficient number of monitors and recorders to simultaneously display and record multiple gaming and count room activities, in addition to recording the views of all dedicated cameras and motion activated dedicated cameras.

101.

Closed Circuit Television (CCTV)

There are more than a thousand CCTV digital cameras in place in many large casinos. In noncasino areas, the digital cameras are pan-tilt-zoom (PTZ) or fixed. They're in areas where they are needed, but not in your face. Discretion is a pervasive concept at all casinos.

The digital cameras on the casino floor are PTZ inside domes or track cameras, allowing for joystick manipulation.

Most hotels have one central monitoring and dispatch area for the hotel and shops; a second one covers the casino. Both monitoring areas operate around the clock, documenting occurrences inside the resort-casino. There are always several monitoring officers on duty at each station.

Security checkpoints, CCTV, alarms, and an access control system separate the public areas of the hotel-resort from its massive back-of-the-house areas. Many of the assets of the property come in and out of back-of-the-house locations. For example, the loading docks receive the goods that are then stored in the shop's inventory warehouse and the hotel's liquor vault, silver rooms, housekeeping supply rooms, and other areas. Money handling and administrative record areas also reside in the back of the house.

To prevent thefts, saturate the warehouse and other stock and money-handling areas with alarm points and CCTV. As in the front of the house, both pan/tilt/zoom and fixed cameras are used. All video transmissions are monitored by officers in the central monitoring station known as the surveillance room.

Access Control

All employees of the hotel or its tenant restaurants and shops are issued magnetic strip photo identification cards by the human resource department in conjunction with security. The cards are programmable, giving human resources and security the ability to allow a level of access designed specifically for each individual.

When reporting for work, all employees must pass through a security checkpoint where an officer ensures that they swipe their ID card to record their entry onto the property. Employees who forget or lose their ID card must be vouched for by a superior before security will let them enter. Vendor employees must also follow a designated route in and out of the casino with several access control points.

102.

Time-Lapse Recorders and Tapes[19]

Over the years, time-lapse recorders have become just as important to managers as CCTV systems. The price for a good one is in the area of $2,000. Considering they are on day and night, twenty-four hours a day, videotapes are a way of gathering the best possible evidence.

Videotapes are sold on the open market from $2 to $12 each. It is recommended that you purchase the very best high quality-grade tape. A standard-grade tape will give you an average image where a high-grade"tape will be more durable, provide sharper images and clearer pictures and will also have less noise and fewer lines, streaks, and white spots.

Videotape is a fragile medium. How can you protect your tapes from damage and maximize their longevity? Here are some suggestions, provided by Surveillance Specialties, Ltd.:

1. Before recording on a tape, fast forward to the end and then rewind in order to relieve stresses on the tape. After viewing the tape, rewind to the beginning for proper storage.

2. Keep videotapes in carefully labeled protective covers.

3. Do not store tapes in areas where they will be exposed to direct sunlight, extreme heat or cold, high humidity, moisture or water.

4. Avoid storing tapes near magnetic fields, such as air conditioners, computer workstations, power panels, stereo speakers and television sets.

5. Do not eject a tape in the middle of a recording or pause tapes for prolonged periods.

6. Have the recorder cleaned and serviced regularly to keep it in top operating condition.

---

[19]From *Physical Security, 150 Things You Should Know*, by Louis A. Tyska and Lawrence Fennelly, Butterworth-Heinmann, 2000, pp. 169–170, and the newsletter for 2000 of Surveillance Specialties Ltd., Boston, Massachusetts.

103.

Surveillance Coverage/ Slot Machines

Common sense would dictate that a slot machine that offers a payout of more than a quarter of a million dollars, or progressives that are around the six-figure mark or even higher, should be monitored by dedicated cameras. These provide coverage of all slot machines affected by that large jackpot, with sufficient clarity to identify the payout lines—in other words, read the reels of the machines.

Now there are computer-linked machines that offer a huge payout. These are often linked by a computer master processor that can tell you when there is a problem, even if there is a door or compartment open. It is still a good idea to keep an eye on the machines.

It would be a good idea to number every bank is numbered and have a large number on top of one of the machines so that surveillance can readily identify the bank number they are looking at. The house number of each machine should be planted clearly and readably on the front of the machine. Ordinarily the house number cannot be read by camera, but a foot trip up there should do it.

So it would be good to have, on a low-denomination slot machine bank of fifteen, cross shots and middle shots, as well as a pan-tilt-zoom (PTZ) on each side of the bank, to give the surveillance investigators the cameras and the shots to work with should any suspicious activity occur.

In other words, your surveillance system should be able to monitor and record a general overview of the activities going on around the slot areas, including the area around the slot change booths where a lot of money, as well as an employee, is housed. This last, of course, links right back to being able to detect internal theft as well as external theft and cheating.

A good idea in a slot area, especially in a larger casino, is to have dedicated cameras recording 24-7 on major aisles and walkways through the slot area. This covers where most of your employee activity takes place, as well as the avenues which the cheat or the scammer may have to take in order to move about the casino freely. There should be enough PTZ cameras throughout the slot areas to be able to follow a suspect or suspects through the casino easily. There should also be a number system on your slot cameras that coincides with the direction that they are moving, in other words, a steady flow of camera numbers in sequential order from a single starting point through the entire casino.

When setting up your surveillance system for your slot area, do not neglect it. Do not pay all your attention to your table games; you must have enough coverage in the slot area to accurately cover everything. You have to understand that slots are the major income for any casino (assuming they have slot machines in their casinos; some states don't allow it). The indicators of slot cheating covered earlier help you to identify the cheats by using this particular coverage.

104.

Table Games

Common sense also dictates surveillance on table games. Obviously you must have the capability to monitor and record, on state-of-the-art equipment, each table game area. In other words, you need pan-tilt-zooms (PTZs) within the pit to use as working cameras, with enough clarity to identify patrons and dealers at the table. Each table game surface should have sufficient coverage and clarity to view the table bank and to determine the configuration of wagers, card values, and game outcome.

There are table games that have progressive jackpots, such as Caribbean stud, let it ride, bonus pai gow poker, and other different types of card games throughout the world. These types of progressive meters should also be covered, in addition to the table itself. It can be a picture in a picture or a whole separate recorder. The purpose is to make sure that the progressions are not stepping up quicker than they should be and that the floor person actually does the proper procedures for the devices on the table. Obviously you should be able to view the table bank and determine the configuration of all the chips in the rack and of course an overall view of the entire table with sufficient clarity to identify your customers as well as personnel. As mentioned, you should have a view of any type of progressive meter, device (such as keypad), jackpot, or special bonus addition to the game.

With most card games, your surveillance must be able to monitor and record each game and each gaming area, just as was previously mentioned. In some areas there is actually a difference between card games and table games.

105.

Keno

Keno is a very popular game but not licensed in many states. In keno the customer will pick a number or combination of from a field of eighty numbers. Twenty numbers are drawn by balls, just like in bingo, with numbers written on the balls, which are blown into the neck of the device and then into the "ears," which are appropriately marked by numbers of the numerical order in which the balls come out. A variety of different devices are used, from the old fashioned spinning cage to more modern computer-driven random number generator. The more numbers that the customer has picked that hit, the more the payoff, depending on the amount of the wager. In essence, it's like a lottery.

The surveillance system must have the capability to monitor the keno balls, the keno ball-drawing device, or, on a lot of properties, the random-number generator. The keno ball-drawing device or the random-number generator should be recorded during the course of the draw by dedicated cameras. It should actually be recorded before and after the draw to make sure that there are no balls left in the device where the balls are housed after they are drawn or in the neck of the device to where they are staged before going into the ears.

A system that helps cover this game—since it depends on the number of customers and the frequency of the draws—is the motion-activated type of equipment, which only records when the games are operating. Of course, this must begin before any balls go into the neck of the device or the random number generators start. There should always be sufficient clarity to resolution identify the balls drawn or the numbers selected.

Your surveillance system should possess a sufficient number of pan-tilt-zoom (PTZ) cameras to covertly observe the activities within the keno area. There should also be fixed cameras over every money drawer where customers or keno runners place the wagers as well as collect the winnings. Coverage should be sufficient to identify the employee performing the different functions as well as to see details of the function itself.

106.

Race and Sports Book

Some licensed gaming establishments have what we call race books and sport books where one can place wagers on various sports, horse races, and dog races, and a pari-mutuel wagering system or other betting system. The surveillance system must be able to monitor and record all general activities in the area. It should cover each writer's station, to clearly see each transaction and wager made; it should also cover the board where betting lines and odds are displayed.

107.

Casino Cage and Vault Areas

The surveillance system should monitor and record a general overview of all activities occurring in each casino cage and vault area with sufficient ability to clearly identify employees within the cage and patrons and employees at the counter. This is done by having cameras positioned with side shots crossing both inside and outside the cage, looking down the customer counter in front of the windows. Cage windows should also be marked so it is clear, either by its paint scheme or by numbers, which window is being viewed. In addition to the two fixed cameras looking down the counter, there should also be a few PTZs just outside the cage area so that you have full pan-tilt-zoom capabilities in case anything occurs just outside as well as inside the cage.

The next issue of importance is to have an excellent camera over each window where transactions are made with customers, so that you can watch and record all transactions as well as see the cash, tokens, chips, and the cash drawer.

In addition to the camera over each window, there should be a fixed camera looking out from the inside with the ability to get face shots of every patron who steps up to the window. A good way to do this would be to set up quad recorders. For eight cage windows, you would utilize just two VCRs and two monitors. Run windows one through four on one monitor and windows five through eight on the next; when you play back you still have a clear view of the patron's face.

When you put together the cross shots inside and outside the cage, the camera over each window, and the face shots of customers who approach the windows, this provides three areas with which you can put a case together, for obvious reasons.

There should also be cameras in the cage that look at all chips, chips storage, keys, keys storage, the manager's station, the main bank area, and safe areas. There should be a couple of PTZs within the cage to give a surveillance operator the ability to look around and see and record all activity that occurs within the cage and to focus in on specific areas.

In the chip fill window, there should be a slip activator, a picture-in-a-picture feature, so that every fill that is released from the cage is recorded. Surveillance should read the fill slip as well as verify the amount of chips being passed out by the cage.

Another area of concern within the cage is your customer safe-deposit-box area. This normally has its own private entrance for the privacy of the customer. The safe-deposit-box, as well as the keys and the transactions, should be well monitored on videotape. The cameras outside looking at doors, and the cameras inside, should be fixed on all doors and entrances coming to the cage. This gives cross coverage of entrances and exits in all of the cage area. Most properties set an amount for high-denomination fills, where it is mandatory for the fill window to notify surveillance when a fill is over a certain amount. This is normally established by the internal controls of the individual property.

All windows to and from count areas, as well as special employee usage windows, should be clearly covered with the same type of diligence that is used by the cage counters.

108.

Coverage of Count Rooms

Hard Count

For the area where coins and tokens from slots are counted, weighed, bagged and wrapped, the surveillance system must possess the capability, with correctly placed pan-tilt-zooms (PTZs), as well as fixed cameras in critical areas, to monitor and record all areas where coin is stored or where the coin is counted. These cameras must be well placed, for there are a lot of areas with large machinery in a hard count room that can be blind spots to the camera if not arranged carefully.

Of course, there must be coverage of all entrances and exits for hard count, just like the cage and all scales used in the count, as well as the wrapping machines and any area where uncounted coin may be stored during the drop and during the count process. Take note that the coverage of scales and counting machines should be very clear in order to view any attempt to manipulate the recorded data taken by the scale, like adding or taking away weight.

There should be phones placed on the outside and inside of the main doors of the count room with direct lines to surveillance. Employees should use these phones to notify surveillance so that it is appropriately logged on the daily activity sheet when anyone exits or enters the rooms.

Another helpful tool at the main entrance to any hard-count room is a scanner device that an employee walks through, like a metal detector, which detects coins on the individual's person. Of course, most count-room employees are supplied with uniforms, jumpsuits that are pocketless, deterring—but not making it impossible—employees from stealing coin or tokens.

Soft Count

In the soft-count room, where paper money from table games and slot-machine bill validators is counted, the system must be able to monitor and record all activities within the soft-count area and connecting rooms, including all doors to the rooms, all drop boxes, all safes, and the storage rack where the table game drop boxes are stored. It's a good idea to have both PTZs and fixed, dedicated cameras in the storage area. A helpful tool in storage areas would be a motion-detector-activated camera.

There should be at least four fixed cameras as well as a few PTZ cameras completely surrounding the counting surface where the employees open the drop boxes. This area should be continuously monitored by both dedicated cameras and the PTZs.

The reason for using both cameras is that it takes a number of employees to get the count done in a limited amount of time. Most internal controls dictate that the count team member, when opening the box and emptying it on the table, must show the inside of the box to at least one camera by holding it up and displaying it with the door open. The surface on which the money is laid should be clear, so you can see underneath the table for any type of activity that could invite theft. The counting surface, for obvious reasons, is continuously monitored by dedicated cameras as well as PTZs.

The surveillance system for the soft count area should be able to monitor and record all areas where the currency is sorted, stacked, counted, and verified, including all count machines and meters. Coverage of all currency counting and sorting machines is strongly recommended; coverage must be sufficiently clear to view its use, especially the input, output, and reject areas.

109.

The Security Detention Room

The security office where people would be detained or where they go when a complaint is being filed should have both video and audio recording. This is to protect both the person brought to the detainment area and the officers who escorted the individual. It helps eliminate a lot of false allegations.

This room should be recorded by both security surveillance and the casino surveillance system as a backup, and both should use both video and audio. It is important to have a sign clearly posted within this area indicating that the area is under both video and audio surveillance.

When a person is detained or brought in for any questioning by casino personnel within this office, it should be recorded. A person is considered to be detained when that person cannot leave on his or her own free will—in other words, the property is depriving the individual of the ability to leave voluntarily. The camera coverage should clearly show the area where the individuals are detained, such as a bench. On the wall behind this bench should be attached a substantial pad so that the individual cannot hurt themselves on the wall. There should be velcro restraining devices that cannot harm the person being physically detained.

This is one of the casino's highest liability areas, where many lawsuits are begun and won by individuals who have been detained here. It is a good idea to check all local and state laws in the area you are in and determine if private property laws apply.

110.

Storage of Tapes or Other Recording Media

All of your tapes, or any other form of recording media, should be kept for a minimum of seven days.

Any tapes that would lead you to believe that company assets or liabilities may be in jeopardy, because of a certain occurrence that may be on videotape, should be kept probably indefinitely, or for an amount of time designated by the legal counsel for your company or casino.

There are certain areas within a casino for which a state regulatory agency or tribal gaming commission may require that recordings be held for a certain amount of time.

It is a good idea (and required by law in many areas) to have in your surveillance system the capability to produce photos or images from your video and or other recordings, for the purpose of investigation or to make certain areas of the casino aware of particular information.

Each original tape that is removed (checked out) from the surveillance room must be logged. This log must cover the date and time, the tape number, what type of coverage is on the tape or area, who wants it and why, and of course the person signing or initialing for the tape, as well as the surveillance agent that is releasing the tape. This is good practice, for it is a documented trail of the whereabouts of a tape that may be used for evidentiary purposes in a court of law.

It is good when certain moves (such as cheating or theft activity) or areas that have to be brought to the attention of the entire Surveillance department, to make dubs of these types of incidents prior to releasing the original. Your Surveillance room should have a user-friendly dubbing station for this. That way you have your own copy of the areas that have to be investigated or looked into.

Of course, tapes (or other recordings) could only be signed out to the very limited number of people, whose names are documented, with the authority to do so.

When a dub or a temp tape is made or pulled, it should still be signed out on the log and put on what is known as a "hold rack." The tape should have proper documentation on the spine label to say how long a tape should be held, and possibly a case number for additional information, if needed. Temporary tapes are made if you have to pull an original tape for a review; you put the temporary in the original tape's place, then put the original right back in after the review. If you don't have to keep that tape and pull it from the general population, then you put it right back into service. Well, you now have a short amount of time on your temporary tape that should still be maintained for a minimum of seven days. This is the type of tape that you would also hold on the hold rack.

Once you have all your tapes and their assigned designations, and your lists and racks and their separate holding areas, develop a good labeling system. A good labeling system can be operated through a computer or separate machine, to where each spine label has a designated assignment to VCR which corresponds to a matching camera number if the system is completely user friendly.

111.

Maintenance of the Surveillance Room and Its Equipment

Since your VCR and or other types of recording devices are normally operating twenty-four hours a day, seven days a week, these machines have to be serviced a lot more than your normal home machine. You need to have trained technicians in CCTV and video repairs to make repairs of malfunctions in a reasonable time, so as to not damage any assigned coverage.

A systematic maintenance program on all equipment in the surveillance room is highly recommended. You assign a person to go through each VCR, rack by rack, and clean and replace belts, pinch rollers, and other parts that wear out. A date is placed on each VCR to show when it was last serviced. The technician will then go to the next bay or rack or next piece of equipment that needs to be serviced, whether it be another row of VCRs, computers, the fax machine, the copier, or whatever. Every piece of equipment must always be serviced in a timely manner.

Once everything has been serviced, then, of course, you go right back and start over, and it will be clear on each piece of equipment on what date it was last serviced.

This should also be kept in a log book that shows all repairs—when they were done, what the camera, or VCR covered what was done and by whom. This log should be retained for an indefinite period and must be kept in the surveillance room.

Dust is a major hazard in surveillance rooms. Regular cleaning and a good air purifier machine within the room will help keep the dust down and out of the VCRs.

Most—about 90 percent—of the cameras in the casino are covered by domes. These domes cannot be cleaned by just anyone; they have to be cleaned by a service technician who is trained on the systems and the type of domes and what needs to be done. It is very easy to scratch one of these domes because they are made from plastics and must be kept very clear. Also, exposed cameras must be gingerly cleaned of dust and other unknown particles. They must be checked at that time to make sure that the shrink wrap on the fittings connecting the cameras is still intact, that the cameras are still pointed and focused correctly, and that they cannot be touched or blocked by anyone or any-thing.

The next piece of work you need to do in maintaining your surveillance system is to make a list sheet of VCRs with camera numbers assigned to them and what the cameras cover: say, VCR #54 using camera #54 covers BJ54. Of course, unless it is numbered this way from the beginning, the system may be a little harder to memorize. It may say camera #54 and VCR #131 for BJ2. So you really have to keep a log of everything, so your operators and technicians, as well as the sheets, are updated constantly.

Now comes the mapping of your system. You need to have a complete map—a big map and small maps for your use and that of your crew—of the casino floor or hotel or whatever type of area you are surveilling. This map should be laid out to show all camera locations and whether they are pan-tilt-zoom fixed. This will help you find camera areas more quickly and efficiently.

If your surveillance system is looking at a casino, and the banks of machines are numbered, then you are able to put those slot-bank numbers on the map as well for an easy cross reference for locating cameras quickly. Table game numbers, shop names, and entrances to critical areas should all be included on the map. These maps should constantly be updated any time a change occurs in the area that you are surveilling.

In many areas, this map is required by gaming laws, and an updated copy must be submitted to gaming regulatory agencies periodically.

112.

Forms and Documentation Utilized During the Daily Operation of a Successful Surveillance Department

1. Sign-in and sign-out log: It should be mandatory that everyone who enters the surveillance room other than surveillance personnel should sign a form listing date, time in and time out, his or her name, the reason for the visit, the affiliated department, if it is internal or external, and the initials or the signatures of the ones visiting the surveillance room. There will be individuals who are exempt from this sign-in and sign-out process, normally a list of these individuals is determined by the surveillance manager or director or above.

2. Tape sign-out log: It should be dictated in the internal policies and procedures who may and may not receive original tapes and dubs. Because evidentiary law may apply to the integrity of any original recording or documentation, this tape sign-in and sign-out log is essential for tape control as well as for maintaining the proper evidentiary trail. This log should include date; time; name; department or agency affiliation, the pertinent information about the tape; the original tape number; shift; the time it is signed in or out; if it is a dub, the dub tape number, the information that is on the tape; the reason for signing the tape out; the initials and or signature of the one signing the tape out; and exactly what is on the tape.

3. Equipment repair and maintenance log: Some states make it mandatory to keep an equipment-repair maintenance log of all surveillance equipment, and some states don't. It is highly recommended that you keep this type of log whether it is dictated by law or not. Accurate documentation of all maintenance or repairs of your surveillance equipment is of utmost importance. An accurate log must be maintained that includes repairs and cleaning of cameras, VCRs, monitors, and all other pertinent equipment, and all duties essential in maintaining an effective CCTV operation.

    Example: VCRs must be constantly maintained to perform their best. A never-ending maintenance program must be established. An accurate log will help keep this maintenance activity data in order, so you can attempt to perform all maintenance before a technical problem has the chance to take its course. Recommended items on the equipment repair and maintenance log are the date the malfunction occurred or the maintenance takes place, who reported it, who is requesting the maintenance or repair, what the problem or scheduled maintenance is, if back-up coverage was needed and if so, what cameras or VCRs, how long the equipment was out of service, a sign-off area for the technician performing the repairs or scheduled maintenance, the type of repair or maintenance that was performed, the date the repair was completed, and the date the equipment was reported put back into service.

4.   The tape repair and replacement log: There will be numerous times when a tape or VCR will malfunction, causing necessary replacement of the tape, VCRs, or both. When this happens and a supplemental tape is required, a temporary tape (temp) must immediately be used. The temp must be accurately labeled on the spine, with date and tape assignment as well as how long it is to be kept. The original tape replacement must be housed in an area specifically designed as a hold rack. The date when the tape may be put back into service or destroyed must be logged. As was mentioned earlier, certain tapes are kept for a certain amount of time. Recommended entries for this type of log are date, time, the assignment of tape to be replaced, the VCR assignment, the location of the original tape—whether it is hold rack, evidence, destruction, file, etc.—when the tape may be released or destroyed, the initials on who released the tapes and to whom, or who placed the temp into service, and the reason why, for example, "back in rotation," "destroyed," or "in evidence."

113.

Monitor Board Set-up and Display

Casino surveillance rooms vary in size, shape, and equipment. Depending on the size of your property, you may work in a broom closet or you may enjoy a room the size of a football field. You may have a state-of-the-art system or you may have inherited a system one step above the old catwalks. Regardless of the size of your room or the state of your system, you will, at the very least, have monitors and cameras. Proper set-up and display of your monitors and cameras will allow you to operate proactively and effectively.

Proper set-up and use of your equipment will provide you the video information you require to operate effectively. Effective operation in a surveillance department (protecting the assets of the property) consists of the following:

1.   Consistent live detection of internal and external theft, fraud, cheating, advantage play, and violation of policy or procedure.

2.   Consistent detection of internal and external theft, fraud, cheating, advantage play, and violation of policy or procedure through review and investigation.

Successful surveillance directors will set up their cameras and monitor display to address the needs of the property. It;s important to identify what those needs are, assign priorities, and determine the most efficient use of your equipment to address those needs.

Consider a casino that has single- and double-deck hand-held games with liberal rules and high table limits. This same casino is located in an area that has a lot of transients and street people who often loiter in the casino. More than likely, this casino will experience frequent visits to their hand-held games by advantage players and card cheats. It will also experience a large number of thefts from their slot customers, such as coin bucket and purse thefts.

This casino's surveillance director expects and plans for such activities. His or her monitor display reflects that planning. He or she places cameras on the vulnerable hand-held games and displays these games live. He or she monitors and evaluates the play on these games continuously. He or she also places cameras in strategic positions within and around the slot areas to detect and monitor suspect individuals. These cameras are also displayed live. Using this system in this fashion, the surveillance director has dramatically increased the chances of detecting suspicious activity in table games and in the slot areas (his or her identified loss or risk areas). He or she is operating proactively. Additionally, should the surveillance director miss an incident that does occur (and we all do) he or she can, in most cases, review the tape and either locate the incident or identify who's responsible.

Monitor set-up and display should be dictated by the needs of the property, experience (types of crimes and losses), and informational flow (game statistics, variance reports, player win-loss reports, etc.).

Your first step consists of identifying vulnerable, high-risk, and critical areas.

1.   Where are you losing?

2.   What and where are you leaking?

3.   What assets are exposed to loss?

The answer to these questions will direct you to your potential or existing loss areas.

Typical casino leaks, losses, and risk areas usually consist of one or more of the following:

1.   Individual or overall table games not holding as expected.

2.   Individual slot machines, type or denomination of slot machines and/or overall slot hold is lower than expected.

3.   Lower than expected revenue from profit centers (food and beverage, retail).

4.   Consistent and reoccurring theft from casino guests.

Let's look at how we can address losses in table games. First of all, the accounting department issues a daily statistical report that details win-loss figures for each table game and for all table games combined. This report lists win-loss figures for each table game and overall table games by the day, month to date, quarter to date, and year to date. If you're not receiving this report already, you need to find out who is issuing it and how to get it; it's critical to your efforts to protect the property.

Daily statistics detail what was won or lost by specific table, game type, and shift, and for all three shifts for the previous day. Surveillance should be aware of any significant wins or losses that occurred. If not, these losses should be researched to ensure they are legitimate (see player evaluations). What we're looking for at this point are losses that are occurring over a longer period: month to date, quarter to date, and year to date. Table wins and losses can be very volatile; you can expect your win percentage to rise and fall, sometimes drastically, in the short term. However, when you look at the win percentage monthly, quarterly, and yearly, it should be in the normal range. If not, something is wrong. If surveillance can't account for the low win percentage (possibly due to an unusual and significant loss to a player or number of players), then you have identified a loss area that requires observation and investigation by the surveillance department.

Surveillance must begin isolating the loss to a specific shift, table, pit or type of game. Once isolated, your monitor set-up should be adjusted to display the game or area to begin your investigation.

Case File

A casino's craps win percentage, over a period of several months, dropped from a solid 15 percent to 17 percent to an unacceptable 11 percent to 12 percent, although handle remained about the same. Initial investigation determined that the rules and table conditions hadn't been changed and that the craps pit hadn't suffered any large losses or unusual play. Surveillance attempted to isolate the problem to a particular game or shift by analyzing the game statistics but was unable to do so. It appeared to be an overall drop in win for no apparent reason.

The surveillance department adjusted its monitor set-up to display each craps game and an overview of the crap pit at all times. Surveillance personnel were assigned to monitor the play and activity occurring on the games and within the pit.

Observation determined that the dealers were taking and paying correctly and accurately. Nobody was seen stuffing checks into hidden pockets or handing checks off to players. Fills, credits and marker transactions were performed properly. Everything surveillance looked at appeared normal. Yet the win percentage remained low.

Finally, a surveillance investigator noticed that there were a large number of tokes for the dealers on the game he was watching. In fact, once surveillance began looking, they noticed the same thing happening on all the other crap games. An unusual number of players were "betting for the boys." The players making the toke bets were not the types to normally toke and the types of toke bets they made were above their level of experience.

Further investigation determined that the crap dealers in this casino were making more money in tokes than almost all of the crap dealers in town. It was also found that the crap dealer's tokes began increasing right about the same time the win percentage decreased. While the casino was losing, the crap dealers were making their best tokes ever.

Now the surveillance department had something to focus on. Surveillance began monitoring craps tokes specifically. A shopping team was hired to play on the craps games and let surveillance know what was being said on the games that surveillance couldn't hear. The joint effort by surveillance and the shopping team soon identified why the win percentage had decreased. The craps dealers were "rough hustling" the players (directly asking and directing players to toke and bet for the dealers). The investigation also determined that the management team (box, floor, and even a shift manager) that were supposed to protect the games were, in fact, allowing the dealers to hustle the players for a percentage of the take.

After terminating a number of dealers and management personnel, and implementing tighter controls, the casinos win percentage returned to normal.

This case illustrates how effective a surveillance department can be when it uses available information to identify loss areas, and focus its resources (information gathering, personnel and equipment) on specific areas to obtain information and provide solutions.

Effective Monitor Set-up and Display

1. Effective monitor set-up and display is established and dictated by property needs (existing and potential loss areas), past experience (types of crimes and losses), and informational flow (game statistics, variance reports, player win/loss reports etc.).

2. Identify your high risk, vulnerable and existing loss areas.

    a. Where and what are you losing?

    b. What is exposed to loss?

1. Plan and implement your coverage to address identified areas.

2. Monitor and record areas that

    a. Protect guests, employees and property (entrances, exits, main aisles). Place cameras at each entrance/exit and in main casino aisles. These cameras should be positioned to obtain clear identification shots of patrons and employees entering and exiting the property or walking in the aisles. The reason for this is, when something does happen, even if you don't have tape of the actual incident, you will be able to review your door and aisle tape and more than likely, locate the person(s) involved. Once you know who you're looking for, your chances of solving the case have increased considerably.

b. Are sensitive areas (cage, count rooms and storage vaults). Obviously, these areas should be monitored closely. However, often these critical areas are observed only occasionally or not at all when they are in operation. These areas are exposed to internal theft and should have overviews of the area displayed or at the very least recorded at all times.

c. Are key games such as hand-held twenty-one or baccarat. These games are vulnerable to quick attacks by advantage players, cheats and employees. Display these games live to provide rapid detection of suspicious activity or investigation of unusual losses.

d. Provide information such as that provided by pit overviews or specific casino areas (high-limit slot areas, bards, etc). Camera coverage of these types of areas will greatly assist a surveillance department to detect unusual activities within and outside these areas. Again, when an incident does occur, these cameras will allow surveillance to investigate to determine when it occurred, who was involved, and what the employees were doing at the time of the incident.

e. Are frequently reviewed or requested for review. Games that are frequently reviewed such as roulette should be displayed. This allows surveillance to make a timely response with minimal effort.

f. Are required by state regulation.

1. Monitor set-up and display is for normal and routine operation. It may be changed somewhat for day-to-day, shift-to-shift operations. It can, if necessary, be changed during emergencies.

2. Operators should be assigned working monitors to patrol freely without affecting the display.

3. Increase your tape rotation as much as possible. Not only will it improve the clarity of tape and assist in the maintenance of your recorders, it will increase your ability to go back and investigate incidents that are reported late or that were occurring over a long period. This is a very inexpensive way to improve your detection ability.

Once you establish your monitor set-up and display, it will provide:

1. Maximum deterrence

2. Proactive operations

3. Timely response with minimal effort

4. Identification of suspects for later response

5. Leads for effective investigation

6. Increased rate of detection

114.

Patrol Techniques

The surveillance department is given many duties and responsibilities. Performing these duties and responsibilities successfully requires not only well trained and motivated personnel, but also an effective system of patrol and observation. Establishing and using such a system allows the department to operate proactively and ensures a constant flow of operational information.

There are three main types of observation techniques:

1. Patrol

2. Audit

3. Close Watch

The patrol is for routine, general surveillance. However, it is not performed randomly. It is a systematic observation of all areas requiring surveillance attention. Surveillance officers, when patrolling, check each area thoroughly for indications of theft or cheating, suspicious activity, and violation of policy and procedure by employees. An officer on patrol is much like a police officer walking a beat; he or she checks to make sure doors are locked, looks in store windows and on the street for suspicious activity, confronts suspicious or out-of-place individuals, and investigates and confronts anything unusual.

Surveillance officers walk their beat with a camera. They patrol their assigned beat or sector with their cameras. They check to ensure that activities within their area are normal, that employees are following policies and procedures, that there are no indications of theft or cheating, and that there are no unusual or suspicious individuals or situations.

An effective patrol technique is the IOU patrol. IOU stands for identify, observe, understand, and describes the patrol functions performed by surveillance officers as they check their assigned areas.

Establishing and Implementing the IOU Patrol

1. Assign individual officers specific areas to monitor such as table games, slots, money-handling areas, etc. Depending on your operation, some areas can be combined and assigned to one officer. For example, slots, cage, and points of sale may be assigned to one officer while another monitors table games and

keno. Note: if only one officer is on duty, he she should use the IOU patrol; however, the higher-risk areas should be given priority and patrolled first and most frequently.

2.   Officers begin their patrol by selecting a reference point to start and finish their patrol of a specific area. For example, an IOU of table games may begin and end at BJ-1 in pit one. A slot IOU could begin in slot section one and end when the last slot section is patrolled.

3.   Identify—The assigned surveillance officer's first step is to identify (with his cameras) each player, guest, and employee in the area or on the game, and also the status of the game at that time. For example, in table games, on a specific table, the officer should place his or her camera on each person on the game including the dealer, for three to five seconds. After identifying each player, the officer should scan the amount of checks or cash in front of that player. The officer should then scan the table tray to illustrate and record the amount of checks in the tray. Finally, he or she should scan the game number for later identification. In other areas, such as slots or the cage, where specific location identifiers may be unavailable, the officer should include enough of the area to allow identification.

4.   Observe—The officer's second step is to establish tri-shot coverage (see camera techniques) and observe the game. He or she should observe for indications of cheating or theft, advantage play, and violations of policy or procedure.

5.   Understand—The officer must "understand" the activity he is observing prior to moving on in the patrol. This simply means that 1) he or she can identify the activity as normal, without any indication of theft cheating or violation of policy or procedure, and has identified the method of play as a nonthreat or 2) the officer has identified the activity as suspicious because he or she is unable to determine the nature of the activity or method of play (see player evaluations), or has detected violations of policy or procedure or indications of theft or cheating.

6.   When an officer has determined the activity is normal and has completed each element of the IOU patrol, he or she may move onto the next table or area and continue the IOU process.

7.   When an officer detects suspicious activity, or is unable to identify (understand) the activity, he or she must continue to observe the game or area until he or she determines it is a normal activity. If the officer continues to be unable to identify the activity as a nonthreat or he or she has detected indications of theft or cheating, he or she must now initiate the appropriate re-

sponse (see response techniques). Note: the detection of a policy or procedure violation often indicates that theft or cheating is occurring. In fact, in almost all incidents of theft or cheating, there can be found a policy or procedure violation, committed intentionally or unintentionally by the employee. Thus, a detected violation should be treated as an indication of theft or cheating until proven otherwise.

8. The IOU patrol and observation of a specific game or area may take only a few minutes or a few hours. For example, the game may not have any players or only players with minimal action. In these cases, the IOU can be performed quickly if suspicious activity is not detected. However, under the same conditions, the officer may detect indications that the dealer is stealing checks, that a player is counting cards, or that a player is winning consistently for unknown reasons. Such an observation could require that the officer maintain coverage indefinitely. It is important to note that when an officer locates suspect activity requiring his undivided attention, this is where the officer should be, protecting the property from existing or potential loss. This is, in fact, the entire purpose of the IOU patrol.

The IOU patrol provides a systematic and thorough method of patrol that allows the surveillance department to work proactively. Used properly, it will provide consistent detection of illicit activity and a constant flow of valuable and pertinent information. Additionally, when an incident does occur that is not detected live, the ability to investigate such an event is greatly enhanced by the identification shots of players and employees in the area and the status of area conditions (table tray amounts, subjects in and around the game, etc.) provided by the videotape of the IOU patrol.

115.

Audit Observation

An audit observation is used to observe and monitor a specific person, area, or department for an assigned period for the purpose of detection of violation of policy or procedure or cheating, theft, or fraud. Audits are assigned routinely to monitor the various departments under a surveillance department's protection or are assigned due to information received from an informed source or from statistical information.

As a surveillance technique, audits are a valuable tool. Performed properly and in conjunction with other surveillance techniques, audits will provide consistent detection of policy and procedure violations and illegal activity, as well as a constant flow of information. Audits are part of routine surveillance operation. Like the IOU patrol, it should be a daily function assigned to a specific investigator and to each shift.

Ideally, each surveillance department would have enough staff to assign one officer on each shift to conduct audits of various departments and individual employees. However, most surveillance departments do not have high enough staff levels to assign their personnel to such specific functions. Departments with smaller staffs, those with just one investigator on duty on each shift, can still perform regular audits and increase both their investigative and detection levels.

The surveillance department must conduct audits to:

1. Ensure that departments are following policy and procedures.

2. Detect external and internal cheating, theft, and fraud.

3. Establish a high level of deterrence.

4. Provide a consistent flow of information for present and future investigations.

Surveillance directors should assign audits to observe:

1. Table games, keno

2. Slots

3. Cage

4. Beverage outlets

5. Food outlets

6. Retail operations

7. Back of the house

Essentially, all operations, transactions, and departments that may affect the profitable operation of the property should be audited routinely. Earlier we discussed why surveillance must conduct audits. Each of the reasons specified is fundamental to effective and proactive surveillance operation. Let's discuss these reasons and why they are important. We will also illustrate their value to the department and property.

1. Ensure that departments and their employees are following policies and procedures.

   In almost every case of cheating, theft, or fraud there is a violation of policy or procedure committed by the employee. The violation may be intentional or unintentional, but it will, more than likely, be there. Remember most casino policies and procedures were developed after cheating or thefts occurred and were implemented to prevent the same type of crime from reoccurring. Employees who do not follow established policies and procedures are providing an opening for themselves and others to commit illegal activities.

   Now that we know that our policies and procedures are critical to the success of each department and to the property, we must ensure that they are strictly followed.

2. Detect external and internal cheating theft and fraud.

   Routine audits of a department by surveillance will detect employees within that department who are not following policy and procedure. This may be due to lack of proper employee training or misunderstanding of the procedures, or the employee simply does not care if he or she abides by the rules or not. It can also indicate the presence of illegal activity.

   Once a policy violation is detected, surveillance must investigate to determine the reason behind the violation of policy or procedure. For example, during an audit of the twenty-one dealers, an investigator observed that one dealer consistently exposed his hole card when placing the card underneath his up card. Further investigation determined that the dealer was new and he was not following procedure because he had not been properly trained. When surveillance reported this observation to the pit, the dealer was given additional training to correct the problem.

In another example, during the audit of a beverage department, surveillance observed a bartender who frequently failed to give customers a receipt after their purchase. Continued observation of the bartender determines that the reason he was not giving receipts is that he was not ringing up each transaction as required. Not only is a receipt not generated without a transaction, but failing to enter a transaction allowed the bartender to steal the money received from the customer to pay for the drink. Further, because the transaction was not entered into the register, no record of the sale existed. The bartender was able to steal without fear of being caught due to his purposely failing to follow procedures. However, because surveillance conducted the audit, he was detected, an investigation was conducted, video evidence was gathered, and he was confronted and later arrested for embezzlement.

3. Establish a high level of deterrence.

    The surveillance department that conducts audits will establish a high level of deterrence. This is because audits will detect policy and procedure violations by employees and criminal activity by both employees and outsiders. Simply put, the word gets around that the surveillance department is very good at catching employees who fail to follow the rules and employees or outsiders who attempt to cheat or steal from the property.

    A positive result of routine surveillance audits is that employees will eventually tend to abide by the policies and procedures. This is due to the employee's perception that it is likely they will be observed by the surveillance department and disciplined. When employees follow the rules, not only is criminal activity deterred, but also the property functions more efficiently and profitably.

    For example, slot jackpot and fill procedures are required to be very strict in order to prevent the theft of company funds. These procedures usually require that at least two, if not more, employees witness and verify that the jackpot or fill is legitimate and the funds are paid out or placed into the slot machine properly. However, slot employees are often busy and sometimes do not verify the jackpot or fill as required. In fact, slot employees who are supposed to act as witnesses frequently do not verify that a jackpot is actually a jackpot or that a fill was actually placed into a machine. Many cases of internal theft have occurred because the witness just signed the jackpot or fill slip without walking over to the machine and personally verifying it as required. Their failure to do so allows employees working singly or with agents to simply take money for the jackpot or the coins or tokens needed for the fill.

A properly performed audit of the slot department by the surveillance department will quickly detect these violations of procedures. Once surveillance reports that some slot employees are not properly verifying fills and jackpots, (normally required by a properties internal control and by the local gaming board), and these employees are disciplined, other employees will follow the rules more closely.

Continued and regular audits of the slot department will ensure that slot employees continue to adhere to their policies and procedures. Their perception is that they will be observed by surveillance and reported. Thus, a high level of deterrence has been established.

4. Provide a consistent flow of information for present and future investigations.

A major benefit of performing audits is that the audit provides consistent information. Information such as whether a department is following procedures is important when you are trying to find out the reason for a drop in win percentage, especially if your general manager is asking you for answers. Even information picked up in the audit that two slot employees appear to be particularly close (possible coconspirators in internal theft) could assist you in the current audit or a later audit.

Audits often start out as routine observations. However, once the audit begins, investigators usually detect something that appears suspicious or unusual enough that it will lead the investigator to focus on specific individuals, policies, or procedures. In many cases, the activity may not have anything to do with the original reason for the audit. But because the audit was being conducted, other information was generated that provided the investigator clues to another, more significant, activity.

Case History

In a recent case, an investigator was performing a routine audit of the casino gift shop. He noted that one of the clerks was wearing a T-shirt that was available for purchase in the shop. The other clerks on duty were wearing the uniform shirt provided by the property. Determined to find out how the clerk had obtained the shirt, he began review of the videotape made during the audit.

His review located the clerk taking the shirt off the rack and walking out of the store without purchasing it. He also found other clerks doing the same thing. In fact, almost every clerk in the store was found on tape removing stock from the store without making any payment.

The audit was initially set up to observe the clerks at the register to ensure they performed their transactions according to procedure. During the audit, it was noted that the clerks were following procedures properly and all appeared routine. However, because of one investigator following up an observation that he felt was unusual, a whole new avenue of investigation was revealed and criminal activity was detected.

Continued observation and investigation determined that the clerks were taking tremendous amounts of stock ranging from cigarettes and candy bars to expensive clothing articles. On occasion, the clerks just handed items out the front doors to waiting associates!

The surveillance department identified each participant and clearly documented his or her activities on videotape. Ultimately, almost the entire crew of clerks was arrested. Further investigation determined that the clerks had been selling the stolen items on the street at a tremendous discount.

Follow-up investigation by the surveillance department ascertained that gift shop management had no idea that they were missing inventory to such an extent. Unbelievably, there was not an inventory control system in place. Management simply replaced items on the shelves and racks as needed. Sales records and inventories were not checked, and inventory audits were never performed.

Needless to say, gift shop management, including a vice president, was promptly fired.

This routine surveillance audit resulted in the arrest and conviction of eight clerks and the termination of three managers. More importantly, it stopped internal theft that cost the property thousands of dollars in merchandise and revenue from sales.

Surveillance audits are probably the most effective technique used by a surveillance department. The audit's ability to detect activities that are harmful to a casino property, establish a deterrence level, and generate necessary information is unparalleled. Use of an audit system will immediately improve the surveillance team and its rate of detection.

Audit Procedures and Techniques

1. Audit each department regularly and routinely. Try to audit different areas and departments each week, if not more often.

2. Begin each audit of a department by observing how policies and procedures are performed. Surveillance must have a current procedural manual from the department being audited.

3. Plan to spend at least one to seven days on each audit. It will often require substantial time to obtain the whole picture of what is occurring. For instance, an audit of slot jackpot and fill procedures may require at least seventy-two hours to ensure that all slot employees are following the proper procedures.

4. Monitor key or vulnerable activities, policies, or procedures. Often this means "follow the money." An audit of the slot department could consist of monitoring fills and jackpots from their point of initiation to their termination at the machine. An audit of a bar would entail observing the purchase of a drink by a customer, the placement of the cash into the register by the bartender, and the return of the receipt to the customer.

5. Upon detection of violation of policy or procedure, cheating, theft or fraud during an audit, continue the audit until you have resolved the issue or have gathered enough evidence to prosecute the individuals. Do not hesitate to add additional investigators, resources, or time to an audit once you have detected suspicious activity.

6. Keep audits confidential. Do not inform anyone other than the surveillance staff that you are conducting an audit, unless they have a need to know. Remember that if you inform a department head that you are performing an audit of his or her department, he or she may leak the information to the employees to make the department look better. It is also in the realm of possibility that department heads and supervisors may be involved in illegal activities occurring within their departments.

7. Do not attempt to obtain department records or other information such as slot fill reports or register transaction reports during the audit unless it is absolutely necessary. Once these records are obtained from an outside source (the department being audited, the accounting department, etc.), you can expect that word of the audit will leak out. Normally, it is wiser to obtain as much videotape and information as possible before asking for outside assistance. Sometimes this is impossible, but make every effort to keep the audit confidential while you are conducting your investigation.

8. Report results of the audit to the appropriate levels of management. Do so even if no detection of exceptions to policy or procedure or illegal activity was found. A report from surveillance stating that the audited department performed at an outstanding level will be well received. It will also

the next audit that has negative results will be given priority attention. The surveillance department will gain a reputation of being fair and even handed.

9. Follow up as soon as possible any audit that results in changes in department policies or procedure or that results in serious consequences such as terminations or arrests. If necessary, audit the department again. This is done to ensure that the detected activity has ceased and that the department is functioning properly.

116.

Close Watches

The final observation technique used by surveillance is the close watch. The close watch is used to monitor a specific individual or group of individuals often for long periods of time. It differs from the audit observation in that it is normally initiated because of some type of information received from an outside source or generated internally by the surveillance department and that it is maintained until the subject of the close watch is proved innocent or guilty.

The close-watch technique is usually successful. This is primarily due to the validity and the specific information obtained. For example, close watches normally require a specific assignment and dedication of resources: time, staff, and equipment. Frequently, covert cameras and equipment are also required.

Section I:
Security Management

117.

Training

As a rule, officers must successfully complete a list of training courses before the end of their probationary period. Training for both proprietary and contract security officers includes casino operations, report writing, patrol routes, basic law, arrest law, handcuffing techniques, use of force, first aid, CPR, and water rescue. Training also includes public relations and diplomacy, which is stressed as the preferred tactic whenever possible.

Additional and advanced security training should be ongoing with the help of the local law enforcement agencies. Local police should work hand in hand with private security to upgrade proficiency through training. All of the officers should be schooled in loss prevention with the aid of local police.

All security officers should be trained in CPR, water rescue, and first aid, including the use of portable defibrillators. Instruction is carried out by several proprietary senior medical trainers. Also, some hotels have as many as 15 regular emergency medical technicians (EMTs).

Patrolling is broken into zones, with officers assigned to one zone per shift. All officers are cross trained to serve in every zone, which includes parking lots, outside waterways, the hotel spa, and back of the house areas such as warehouses, administrative areas, and loading docks. It is important to train your officers in all respective areas that they are responsible for.

Training, Training, Training

It seems that much time is spent on training of new employees. However, this is much needed and an absolute must if you want an effective, trained, and well educated staff.

From table games, cage, slots, and general surveillance to everything else, it just seems that persons cannot learn required knowledge fast enough. But we have to be patient and wait until they are ready to take on the tasks at hand.

Our recommendation to all is to be patient and create a good training program. From the new employees to the well seasoned ones, everyone should receive constant training. There is always some new technique being used to cheat machines and table games that we all have to be aware of in order to detect it.

Training is a must have. And employees like to learn new things that deal with their professions.

Use the classes and seminars provided in this industry. That is why they exist. Who knows, you might learn something also.

118.

Liaison

With regard to security's relationship with local law enforcement, many security directors couldn't be more pleased. There is no antagonism on either side. We know we're here for the same purpose.

Indeed, police rely on the private security forces to keep their houses clean. As big as the police force sometimes is, private security is many times larger—a fact recognized by both the public and private facets of law enforcement. The groups should exchange updates and network at monthly meetings that include representatives from all police units involved with tourist security and safety.

119.

Patron Protection

Although security is integral to the protection of money and the recognition of cheaters, one of security's primary duties on the casino floor is to keep an eye out for patrons. Officers are continuously patrolling, looking for potential victims.

The most prevalent crimes on the casino floor are those carried out by the opportunistic criminal. Women, for instance, sometimes leave their purses at a slot machine when they move off to play other games. The consumption of alcohol also makes patrons forget to safeguard their valuables.

At many hotels any employee who works in areas where alcohol is served is trained to recognize problem drinkers and anyone who is past their point of rational judgment. When a casino patron has had too much alcohol, security officers gently and tactfully step in. "We try to get the person to his or her room, or we put them in a taxi to wherever they reside." Even in cases when inebriated patrons become aggressive and threatening, security tries to take a quiet approach.

120.

Guest Protection

Security in the hotel tower begins on the main level and lobby with checkpoints at the elevators, where guests must show electronic room keys and vouch for any nonguests in tow. In addition, there is a continuous crisscrossing of officer patrols inside the hotel tower. All officers create an electronic record of their tours by swiping a magnetic stripe card through readers mounted at various locations along the route.

The guest room door locks can aid security with a printout of the times of any entries; the electronic keys also store a record of the times and locations of any key's use. In addition, all guest rooms are equipped with an in-room safe specifically designed for the laptop computers that are the prime pickings of today's hotel room burglars.

When celebrities reside at the hotel, security will consult with the VIP staff to create an effective, comfortable level of security. Security escorts can be assigned to accompany the celebrity when he or she is on the property. If needed, hotel floors or sections of floors can be blocked off, or security officers can be stationed at elevators to make sure that no one who is not a key-carrying guest for that level arrives on that floor. Officers can also be posted at the door to the VIP's suite.

Security managers regularly check bookings to find out if there is anyone coming who has any type of status that might be of concern to security. Often, however, celebrities want to remain anonymous. If so, security can provide plainclothes escorts or any other low-key security services that the VIP might request.

121.

Protection of Guests Inside the Hotel

Protection of guests from thieves and scam artists should be a primary concern of not only the security staff but all casino and hotel employees. One guest who gets ripped off in your casino will tell his or her story, and others who hear about it, even third and fourth hand, will avoid a place where someone they know of got ripped off. This is a loss of future income.

People are careless. Any walk through a casino, hotel, or shopping mall will reveal women being careless with purses and bags, men draping jackets (with wallets, etc., in the pockets) over the backs of seats, people leaving valuables unattended. These are the targets of distract thieves.

Foreign nationals are preferred targets of thieves and scam artists. The thieves know that even if they are caught, a foreign national is unlikely to return to this country to testify in a trial.

A trained operator soon learns to pick out of a crowd those people who are not there for entertainment. They walk differently; they are alert and looking at different things. Investigators should learn to trust their instincts on this. It cannot hurt to watch someone just because you don't like his looks.

Hotel check-in areas, bell desks, and valet areas are common target areas. People coming in are tired from traveling and easily distracted. People leaving are in a hurry and often hung over. These areas should be scanned often, especially at busy times, for known or suspected thieves.

Your hotel staff, as well, are potential thieves. Though this does not happen as often as guests claim, money and other valuables left in a room are obvious targets of maids, bellmen, and other nonstaff people who come into the rooms, including prostitutes.

Cleaning staff are also occasionally suspect. A bucket of coins or a purse left unattended can be a big temptation for a porter.

When a purse is reported stolen or missing from the casino floor, often a quick check of wastebaskets in the area, or the nearest restrooms (both genders), will locate at least the bag or wallet with ID and sometimes credit cards intact. Many thieves are only interested in the cash, knowing that attempting to use stolen credit cards is a quick way to get caught and also carries a much heavier penalty. It is also a good idea to check the waste bin that any porters are using.

Reported thefts of items from rooms, such as jewelry, cash or other valuables, should prompt a quick check of maid carts and the areas where they are stored.

Housekeeping Supervisors should be alert for missing keys and also should watch out for people inspecting maid carts. Housekeeping passkeys should be attached to the room attendants' bodies or clothing, never left on carts.

Prostitutes are among the most common hazards in a resort town. Male guests, away from their wives for a weekend, or in town for conventions, are often the victims of prostitutes who have no problem with a bit of theft on the side. It is income they don't report to their pimps. And the guests often don't even report it, fearing that word will get back to their wives. ("Honey, what was that summons to Las Vegas court that was in the mail today?")

Busy holiday weekends, with hundreds of thousands of people in town, are the annual income producers for organized thieves. They are more easily lost in the crowds, security staff and police are often too busy to be completely alert to their presence, and the crowds themselves mask the activities and presence of teams of people intent on theft.

A large crowd around a table with relatively little play can be an indicator of an organized distract team, especially if one of the players is displaying a lot of money. Often a distract team has five or more people, each fulfilling a separate function. (This can also indicate a cheat team, such as past-posters; however, with a past-post team, most of those there will also be "players.")

Be suspicious of anyone dressed in clothing that approximates any uniform of the hotel or casino. Counterfeit "floor people" in the slots area are a favorite scam, and a very effective one. Slot or pit personnel should be able to report such an occurrence, and any other suspicious characters or activity, to surveillance or security, without fear of having their reports belittled or ignored.

Certain types of slot machines attract scam artists. These are any machines that have an element of predictability about when they will pay off, such as a screen that shows an accumulation of symbols that, when the full, pays a jackpot. Be aware of these slot banks, and scan the areas often for people who reappear time after time. They will often be running a "let me show you how this works" routine.

Use your pit personnel to help protect the guests from their own carelessness. Call the pit and let them know that "the guest on seat 5 of BJ 28 has her purse looped over the back of her chair." Prevention is much better than filling out paperwork and reports. If a theft can be prevented with a few words to the guest, that leaves that much more time for the floor person to watch the games. Also, it is very hard for a guest to have fun when all their credit cards and cash have been stolen.

Surveillance staff should know the casino and hotel areas as well as the walk-around security people. They need to be able to track suspects, be able to predict where someone will go next so they can follow with cameras. Often a distract team or other group knows the casino as well as the staff, having previously scouted it, and they have often drilled their escape.

Be alert for people who are seen continually looking at or into the cameras. They are searching for areas of no or poor coverage.

Other Hazards

Certain areas should have cameras recording full time. These are escalators, entry doors, stairways, and others. Certain hazards such as wet floors, crowds, and so on, occur at these areas.

Surveillance and security should also keep their eyes on cleaning staff in the hotel and casino. Careless or ignorant cleaners do silly things: They stretch vacuum cords across pathways, even across stairway and escalator entries. They leave wet spots, hang off the edges of projections, and stand in high places with no support. These are hazards to guests and staff. Your best protection in this case is prompt reporting of such hazards to security and housekeeping, and effective correction of the individuals involved.

122.

Protection of Guests Outside the Hotel-Casino Complex

The first thing to remember is that anyone with large amounts of cash or valuables is a potential target.

High-roller guests, carrying cash out of the hotel, should be offered a security escort, especially if they are traveling in their own vehicle. Better yet, cage or casino hosts should offer electronic transfer as an option.

Protection of the names and addresses of hotel and casino guests should be absolute. This means computer security. No one who has not been authorized to do so as a specific part of their job functions should be allowed to give away or sell or even access the names or other data regarding the hotel guests.

Just imagine what an organized group could do if they could access information regarding high-end players. First, they would know when potential targets would be coming to the hotel, so they could organize thefts from the targets' homes. Second, if they could find out in advance what rooms the guests would be staying in, thefts on hotel premises could be arranged and planned in advance. If criminals can predict (from casino records) when and where a person would be playing, they know when the room or suite might be unattended, and they could even plan in advance how to arrange a theft of cash from the person in the casino.

Certain types of gatherings, such as jewelers' conventions, Indian shows, rodeos, and so on, attract people with lots to steal. Security should be beefed up at these times, and camera surveillance should be increased both in the convention area and other areas that offer targets of opportunity, such as hotel check-in, valet, shopping areas, who has not been authorized to do so as a specific part of their job functions and others.

Many guests arriving in tourist destination towns are sadly misinformed as to the degree of protection actually available. They assume that there is sufficient police presence to discourage thieves, scam artists, and others. Unfortunately, this tends to make them careless with their property. They are on vacation, they don't want to worry, but it is impossible to stop all the thieves before they act.

A briefing sheet could be given to every hotel guest, telling them the simple things they could do to avoid becoming the victims of the various scams. Things like, never leave your purse or money unattended, don't carry all your money with you, don't leave your expensive jewelry sitting out on the hotel-room dresser, lock your car in the parking garage, and other common-sense pointers that people don't follow. We have all seen that the greatest majority of victims, to some degree, brought it on themselves by their own carelessness. This can be prevented.

Other Hazards:

Major hazards to tourists include high-traffic areas, construction, cleaning and landscaping crews at work, and getting to and from the hotel and airports. During conventions, travel to and from the convention is not just an inconvenience; it can be a hazard to life and property. One of the greatest services that a hotel can offer its guests is regular shuttle service to and from convention areas outside the hotel, including buses, contracts with taxi companies, and company limousines.

High-traffic areas around a casino should be surveyed and analyzed. Is this the best place for a taxi line? Does traffic flow smoothly through the valet area, or are guests forced to walk across vehicular traffic to reach the front doors? Can guests leaving through the front door reach the valet pickup area without walking through a stream of rushing cabs?

Self-parking areas are another major hazard to health, life, and property. Can guests leave the hotel and reach their cars without having to traverse unlighted areas? Is there sufficient (and sufficiently obvious) camera coverage in the parking area to discourage would-be strong-arm thieves? Can people safely walk through the parking garage, looking for where they left their cars, without being run over because of poor visibility? Can a thief walk through the parking area, checking out vehicles, without being seen? Is there sufficient security presence to discourage would-be thieves of all varieties?

A recent scam in Las Vegas involved a group who simply drove a truck into casino parking garages, loaded up Harley-Davidson motorcycles, and drove away. Could this occur at your hotel?

123.

Casino Monitoring

The casinos include tables featuring many different games of chance, including increasingly popular Asian games such as pai gow poker, as well as the better known blackjack, craps, poker, and roulette. There are slot machines of various denominations, a sportsbook, and a keno lounge. A semi-private, high-limit salon includes high-denomination slots, baccarat, and several table games to draw in the premium player.

The gaming area is monitored from the casino's control center, which is staffed by personnel with gaming security backgrounds. The casino camera operators are educated in the forms of cheating and scams associated with each game. To that end, their training is constant, often with the help of local police. Representatives of the gaming control board also visit frequently to provide officers with updates.

Some casinos are getting into the use of facial recognition technology for the casino, and other biometric technologies for the rest of the property.

On the floor, a security booth is prominently situated next to the cage—the area where chips are cashed and other monetary transactions take place. Security controls all entrances to the cage area. Officers also accompany personnel during movements of money anywhere on site, such as when cash must be loaded onto armored cars for bank deposit. In addition, officers escort employees who service the casino during fills, drops, or other money and chip-handling duties.

124.

Dealing With Slip and Fall Incidents

Never assume at the beginning that any slip and fall is a phony one. From the first report of a slip and fall incident, you must assume that it is genuine, and deal with it accordingly.

This means that medical attention must be offered, and if it is declined, then the person must sign a complete release for you. If the person refuses immediate medical attention that you offer, but wants to see their own doctor first, you have a very good indicator of a phony incident.

The process of dealing with phony incidents, however, must start long before any such incidents can occur. High-risk areas, such as stairways, escalators, slick walkways, valet parking areas, and sidewalks that get wet, must be dealt with in such a way that a slip is first of all unlikely, and second, it should be filmed.

Security should have cameras on all high-risk areas, around swimming pools, spas, doorways, and fountains. These should be recording 24-7.

Prevention is the key. If your pool areas and spas are surfaced with high friction concrete, water on the surface will not cause accidents. And if someone falls in these areas, it is easier to show that the company was not negligent, which is always the basis of any lawsuit.

Slick areas such as marble floors must be kept clean, and the cleaning crews must always use proper warning equipment, cordon off wet areas, and never leave areas wet behind them.

Cleaning staff must be properly trained. They must use their equipment correctly and never create unacceptable risks, such as power cords stretched across stairwells and walkways, machines left unattended. All reasonable safety precautions must be taken.

A reputation for dealing honestly and fairly, but never caving in to phony lawsuits, must be created and maintained.

However, sooner or later any company may become the target of an undeserved lawsuit. Dealing with it begins with the first report of a fall, not when the lawyers get together.

Staff must be trained in proper handling of guest accidents. The company lawyers should be able to provide guidelines; they should also provide such things as releases and a checklist of what must be done and what documentation is required.

Security responding to such a report must never report suspicions of a phony fall over the radio. Others besides the officers can hear those reports.

Officers must look for any evidence that the "cause" of the fall, such as spilled liquids, was actually put there by the victim. Pictures should be taken of the actual place where the person's foot slipped, and there should be evidence that the person's foot actually slid. An effort should be made to find out the last time a cleaner went through. For a successful lawsuit to be run against the hotel, negligence on the part of the hotel must be shown by the plaintiff's attorney, and if you can document that the area had recently been properly cleaned, such a claim may be worthless.

In the case of outside falls, such as on a sidewalk where landscaping water has spread, it's a good idea to show, in photos or video, that there was an alternative route—that the victim was not forced to actually walk through the water to reach his or her destination. And if someone slips on an area currently being cleaned, photos and video showing placement of warning signs is good documentation.

Questions of witnesses should determine whether the victim was actually doing horseplay in the area, and it should also be determined whether the person was inebriated at the time. If the person tripped over something, show that they did not in fact have to walk over whatever it was they tripped on.

Document everything about the fall, including the names and addresses of any witnesses. Especially attempt to find staff that saw the incident. Any video footage should be held aside as evidence. Complete statements of the occurrence should be taken from anyone involved, and if several people in the same party are there, separate statements should be taken. These should be filled out in separate areas, or the people should be videotaped while they are doing it, to prevent or record any cross-consultation on the facts.

Whether a person claims to be injured at the time or not, medical attention should be offered. If medical attention is declined, the victim should sign a release.

Complete reports should be filed with documentation from any staff, all witnesses, the EMT, and the medical report itself. File it all, together with any applicable video footage.

125.

Prostitution: The Forgotten Crime

One problem that the casino and hotel industry deals with almost continuously is the oldest profession in the world, prostitution. Crimes of robbery, extortion, blackmail, assault and, yes, even murder, seem to center around prostitution. Frequently organized crime has control of prostitution, although high-profile prostitutes have been known to be managed by entrepreneurs in the entertainment and fashion industries.

The international influence of prostitution is a well established fact. Espionage has made use of both male and female prostitutes to ensnare diplomats into being controlled by foreign powers. Russians, South and Central Americans, and Canadians have been introduced into the cartel prostitution rings around the globe. Japan and the United States are two major receivers of the white slave trade.

The hotel, motel, and casino industries have multiple interests in dealing with the prevention and elimination of prostitution in and around their individual venues. Those interests include the safety of guests and visitors and the elimination of crime.

Expectations of support and assistance from police can be varied. Police control of prostitution can range from rigid control or prevention to no control whatsoever. Therefore, individual hotels and motels must make their own commitment to the prevention or elimination of prostitution or simply safeguarding guests and visitors from its vices in subtle ways.

When a registered patron returns to the establishment with a "guest," it is difficult, if not impossible, to determine the relationship and circumstances. There is a difference when a patron meets the "guest" on hotel property, as opposed to bringing the "guest" back to the hotel. It is essential, therefore, that the security staff, with as much cooperation as it can obtain from local authorities, purges the hotel property of all undesirables, be they male or female.

Dealing with the problem:

How do we deal with this problem and reduce prostitution, protect the corporate reputation and prevent being charged with harassment?

1.   As a rule, prostitutes do not carry identification. This way, if they are arrested, they can give a phony name.

2.   In the event you suspect a potential hooker, stop them, inquire as to what they are up to, and arrest if you have the authority and probable cause or give a trespass warning followed by a detailed report.

3.   Contact the local law enforcement vice unit for assistance. The prostitute will know your security force, but they may not know the vice cops. Some police departments have educational programs and can teach your security force how to spot and how to deal with the problem.

There are several things to be aware of:

1.   The reputation of a "nice family hotel" will be no longer.

2.   Other women will be the first to recognize a prostitute.

3.   If allowed to continue, they will be followed by more, as well as their pimps and drug dealers.

So, the elements described will lead to a bad reputation and a bad environment. Signs to watch for:

1.   The prostitute is a single female or male who orders a drink and walks from man to man carrying on a conversation.

2.   The prostitute leaves with a man and is often back at the bar in less than an hour.

3.   Hookers are very friendly with bartenders and waitresses who help them set up their johns and tip well in return.

126.

Physical Security

Purpose

The purpose of this section is to ensure that baseline physical security measures are in place at all facilities and that the measures in place are auditable and sufficient to assure the protection of assets. These assets include employees, technologies, physical assets, and information related to the conduct of corporate business. The protection of assets is a management responsibility, and it is the responsibility of managers to ensure compliance with these standards.

Public Space

Space designated by the corporation for general access by the public or noncorporate groups (e.g., ground level lobbies, customer centers, comfort stations, etc.) must be designed to prevent unauthorized access after normal business hours.

Interior Space

For the purpose of these standards or guidelines, interior space is defined as space within your facility, or leased or rented space within a shared building, in which the general population may move without access controls. Generally, hallways, office areas, kitchens, and common areas are classified as interior space.

Restricted Space

For the purpose of this section, restricted space is defined as space within a facility, or leased or rented within a shared building, owned by a specific group having a defined business need or function considered critical to the corporation, the facility, or the product. Generally, labs, offices, data centers, executive briefing centers, infant and childcare centers, and utility and mechanical vaults (money areas) are classified as restricted space.

127.

Perimeter Security

Perimeter Lighting

At a minimum, parking lots, loading docks, and ramps must be illuminated during nondaylight hours to enhance employee safety and security and to support CCTV systems where installed. Adequate lighting must be provided during all hours in garages and other covered parking and loading areas to provide for the safety and security of employees.

Employee Parking Garages (Car Parks)

Access to all garages must be restricted to authorized employees who will be identified for each entry. Each entrance and exit must be equipped with vehicle control systems which include at least the following:

1. Electrically operated gates which can be operated by security personnel in a security control center, and badge reader located in a convenient location for a driver

2. Intercom system located in a convenient location for a driver to communicate with the security control center

3. Lighting to illuminate gate area and approaches, and to support CCTV systems

4. Unobstructed view of entering and exiting vehicles via CCTV from the security control center

5. Signs to post property and instruct visitors and unauthorized others

Garages must be equipped with emergency communications systems monitored at the security control center. Access from the garage into buildings must be limited, secure, and well lighted, with concealment areas minimized.

Public Parking Lots (Car Parks)

All parking lots must be posted, indicating property boundaries and entries restricted to authorized persons only.

In addition, parking lots must be equipped with the following:

1. CCTV systems capable of displaying and videotaping parking lot activity

2. Emergency communication systems throughout the parking lot area

3. Lighting to illuminate the parking lot area and support CCTV systems

4. All systems must be monitored by appropriate staff which would consist of:

    a. All personnel

    b. Building security

    c. Staffed security control center

    d. Random security patrols of parking lots

128.

Building Patrol

Responsibilities of Building Patrol

One of the most important duties of a security officer is to patrol the entire complex, including public areas and the workplace. Officers assigned to building patrol duty will patrol all areas of the building and should be on the lookout for the following:

1. Poor safety practices, violations of safety rules, or hazardous conditions not specifically noted in the officer's instructions.

2. Poor fire prevention practices or obstructions to any area that would prevent swift access to fire equipment or fire evacuation.

3. Improper storage or handling of strictly private documents or products. In accordance with standing procedures, strictly private documents should only be confiscated if left out in plain sight. Officers should not look through stacks of paper for such documents. If a strictly private document or product is removed by an officer, a note should be left for the employee to that effect with instructions to contact the security manager to retrieve the document.

4. Defective motors, fans, and all other electrical equipment.

5. Open doors that should be locked and locks that may be open.

6. Defective, misplaced, or missing fire or emergency equipment, including fire extinguishers and first aid kits.

7. Any evidence of insect or rodent pests in any area, or even animals inside the complex.

8. An officer on building-patrol duty should be particularly careful for his own safety. The officer is on patrol to protect others, but most of the time there is no one present to protect the officer. He must, therefore, take care of himself. Note the following suggestions.

    a. Use a flashlight if lighting conditions are not adequate for safe walking.

    b. Use handrails when ascending or descending stairs.

    c.   Observe all safety warning signs and procedures.

    d.   Never assume that fumes are harmless.

    e.   Make note of open doors.

    f.   Make note of all burned out lights.

    g.   Make note of anything unusual.

Vehicle Tours

The outside mobile officer is responsible for, among other things, driving the perimeters of all area buildings and through all parking facilities. When doing an inspection by vehicle, drive slowly enough to be thorough, but not in a manner that endangers either yourself or others. When checking outlying buildings after hours, get out of the vehicle and make sure that the building is secure. Be sure to make note of overnight parking vehicles.

Conclusion

Day after day, hour after hour, the security officer patrols the complex. Then at 3:00 a.m., it is the smell of smoke, or water is rushing out the hallway, or a strange vehicle is seen racing out of the parking lot, and then a door is found open and contents are on the ground from a secured area, or an intrusion alarm has gone off and the officer has to respond. All of the above are action items, by which we mean an incident, a response, a notification, and a report.

129.

Field Notes and Report Writing

A notebook is a very important tool for a security officer. Good notes during an interview or at a crime scene can play a significant role in an investigation that leads to the successful prosecution of an offender. While, realistically, very few incidents actually result in a prosecutable case, you should always make sure that your report is sufficiently detailed to be of value should a legal case be pursued.

Notes taken at the scene from the victim and witnesses represent the original source material employed in writing up the incident report. Along with other related records, they form the basis for any future action to be taken in a given case. A comprehensive incident report is, therefore, essential for investigative follow-up.

While a good memory is a wonderful asset, very few of us have cultivated the faculty to recall all of the details of an interview at a later time. During the time between taking the report and writing it up, essential details can be forgotten if good notes are not taken.

130.

Elements of Field Note Taking and Crime Scene Reporting

Use of a Notebook During an Interview

Interviewing skills are perfected through experience and careful application of certain fundamental principles. The successful officer sells him- or herself and the department by being calm, thorough, businesslike, and friendly. Investigating a crime can entail contact with several groups of persons: complainants, witnesses, and suspects.

In most cases, the approach to all types of individuals should be friendly and helpful rather than formal, overbearing, or officious. Goodwill and excellent public relations, which have taken the department years to establish, can vanish during a poorly conducted interview. One rude or ill-mannered officer can destroy the public respect for his or her fellow officers.

The use of a notebook and how soon it is brought out depends to a great extent on the person or persons being interviewed.

1. The ordinary complainant is not reluctant to talk freely about the case at issue. If the person is emotionally upset, it is better to get a rapid-fire verbal account and then have the story repeated slowly so that adequate notes may be taken.

2. In the case of a witness, an appeal should be made for his or her aid. This can be done using a friendly, businesslike approach. When the witness is sympathetic toward the cause, he or she will probably volunteer certain information. In some instances, you will find a witness will be agreeable to giving a short statement covering his or her knowledge of the offense.

3. A suspect may not talk in the presence of a notebook. Therefore, discuss the issue with him or her and if the suspect commits him- or herself to a story, bring out the notebook and recapitulate the story. There are many instances, however, where circumstances alter the situation and a different procedure may be necessary.

Essentials of Adequate Notes

Notes should reflect an interview that covered completely information regarding the victim, suspect, perpetrator, witness, and owner. When gathering information for an incident report, make sure that all names are complete and spelled correctly, and that the officer's name and telephone numbers are included.

Incident data should be recorded in the notebook clearly, completely, and accurately. Notes should be neat, legible and understandable. Complete notes cover all the details of the crime. When writing a report, keep these six basic questions in mind and cover all of the items that apply: WHO? WHAT? WHERE? WHEN? WHY? HOW?

Who:

1. Who is making the report?

2. Who discovered the loss or crime?

3. Who are the witnesses?

4. Who are the possible suspects?

5. Who took the report?

6. What other people were notified?

What:

7. What occurred?

8. What kind of damage was done, if any?

9. What is the value of the missing property?

10. What is the extent of the damage?

11. What evidence was found at the scene?

12. What action is being taken by you?

13. What further action needs to be taken by others?

Where:

14. Where was the offense committed? Location?

15. Where was the evidence found?

16. Where has a similar offense been committed?

17. Where was the suspect last seen?

When:

18. What time was the offense reported?

19. When was the offense committed? (Time)

20. When was the offense discovered? (Time)

21. When was a similar offense committed in this area? (Date and time)

How:

22. How was the offense committed? (Method)

23. How did the perpetrator gain entrance?

24. How was the offense discovered?

25. How well was the area searched for evidence?

Why:

26. Why did the perpetrator use this method of entrance?

27. Why was this particular item taken?

28. Why was the offense committed at this particular time?

29. Why were certain things taken and not others?

30. Why was there a delay reporting the offense?

The Incident Report

The following are guidelines for filling out an incident report:

1.   The type of incident should be properly identified and indicated on the report.

2.   Be sure that the information on the reporting party includes their telephone number. Remember that the reporting party is the person being interviewed, not the officer.

3.   The first paragraph in the narrative should summarize the facts.

4.   While there are several acceptable formats for the narrative, it is essential that *all* of the pertinent information be included.

5.   The final paragraph in the narrative should indicate where the case stands at the time the report is being written.

6.   Finished reports should be submitted to the supervisor for signature and distribution to management.

Conclusion

It does not matter what area or field of security you are working. A good incident report, well written and prepared, is a must. Supervisors have an obligation to ensure they are done correctly and contain all the necessary elements. In many cases today, reports are generated in computers. The spell check feature has become a way of life. However, the body of the report still has to be prepared and entered into the computer.

131.

Uniforms: The Blue or Gray Blazer vs. the Traditional Uniform

In preparing this section, we discussed the issue with several security administrators who told us the following:

1. I've used blazers as a daily uniform for one reason only—to obtain a safer look. We were looking for the slightly more friendly look with navy blue blazer, white shirt, and tie.

2. We also had the traditional uniform we used during the evening and weekend shifts.

3. Blazer uniforms are a bit limited with respect to duty gear the security officer is required to carry.

4. The blazer with white shirt and tie are ideal for the executive look and appearance as well as the attendance of various meetings.

5. I like the blazer look at ceremonial and specific functions.

6. We have a lot of crime in our shopping mall and need the traditional-uniform look to show authority.

7. When I took over this operation I inherited the blazer look and baseball caps along with low morale, low performance, and low community respect. The traditional uniform was our overall answer. Crime went down and attitudes became positive.

8. "I have concerns," said a well-known security director, "that our protection officers will look like doormen and will lose that authority figure appearance."

9. I think you must look at the many variables: the crime rate, the duties required to be performed, and the effectiveness of the operation. I can't imagine a security officer in blazer directing traffic would be taken seriously.

10. This has been debated for over twenty years and will be for the next twenty.

11. What we are talking about is the security officer's appearance, image, and effectiveness and how it fits in with the site's operation. I've seen security officers in blazers with longer than necessary pants and was told it's a cultural thing. I told the administrator it looks awful and kills the effectiveness and image. Alterations were made to the pants.

Conclusion: So the debate goes on the pros and cons. Baseball hats became part of the uniform because of the television show "Hill Street Blues."

Question: Can the security officer be effective, proactive and forceful in your complex wearing a particular set of uniforms? It's your call.

The hardware and equipment given to security officers should be approved, issued and authorized, and every security officer should be trained and certified in their use.

Sample of Policy of Uniforms and Equipment

The year-round protective services uniform will consist of a blue suit, white shirt, tie, and black shoes. Full-time officers will be supplied with two suits, five shirts, and two ties. Part-time officers will be supplied with one full suit, an extra pair of pants (skirt for females), two shirts, and a tie. All uniforms are to be kept clean and are not to be worn for purposes other than official business. Officers are responsible for ensuring the cleanliness of their uniforms. **An approved name tag is to be worn at all times on the jacket.**

Equipment furnished by the company will be issued to officers by a supervisor, and no items are to be taken without the supervisor's knowledge. While on duty, officers are to wear only the prescribed, complete uniform and equipment.

Uniforms that are damaged or lost in the performance of duty should be reported to the supervisor and will be replaced at no expense to the officer. Should any item be damaged or lost through carelessness of the officer, the repair or replacement will be charged to that officer. Old and worn-out articles of a uniform should be presented to the supervisor for replacement. When an officer leaves the department for any reason, he will immediately return all company property issued. Property not returned may be deducted from the officer's final paycheck at current replacement cost.

All officers are to look and act professional while in uniform and while on duty.

132.

Casino Position Descriptions

Casino Manager:

1.   Institutes and enforces rules, procedures, and regulations.

2.   Safeguards casino's assets.

3.   Responsible for general management of casino.

4.   Has complete authority over all casino personnel.

5.   Approves credit as set by internal guidelines.

6.   Verifies large payoffs. Amount varies according to internal policies.

7.   Supervises and maintains work schedules of personnel.

8.   Usually has authority to offer complimentary services to customers, such as room, food, beverage, and entertainment. Additionally sees to special requests from high rollers, such as a private table or raised betting limit.

Casino Shift Manager:

1.   Safeguards casino assets on his or her assigned shift.

2.   Enforces casino rules and regulations.

3.   Approves credit within guidelines set by casino manager or above.

4.   Attends to customer disputes on assigned shift.

5.   Assigns pit personnel to their designated areas.

6.   Issues all gaming instruments, such as cards and dice, and ensures the integrity of items issued.

7.   Represents the casino manager in his or her absence.

Casino Pit Supervisor:

1. Protects company's assets within assigned pit area.

2. Manages of assigned pit.

3. Enforces rules and regulations within assigned pit area.

4. Attends to customer disputes.

5. Maintains record of table inventories, fills and credits.

6. Issues playing cards and dice following proper inspection and procedures.

7. May offer limited complimentary services to players.

8. Authority over casino floor person(s) and dealers

133.

Victims

Inevitably, there will be times when a guest or patron will become a victim to a crime. To communicate with a victim and obtain all pertinent information, you must first understand the victim's feelings and emotions.

1. A victim is someone who is affected emotionally, mentally, or physically as a result of a crime directed toward them or around them, especially to another family member or friend.

2. Some victims develop an extremely low self-esteem.

3. To help understand a victim, try to put yourself (or a family member) in the shoes of the victim.

4. Do not automatically assume that the victim is the instigator.

5. Victims feel violated.

6. Victims will experience:

    ● Denial

    ● Guilt

    ● Rage

    ● Confusion

    ● Desire for immediate justice

    ● Self pity

    ● Fear

    ● Violation

Always try to be understanding, and be a good listener. Two very powerful words to use while speaking to a victim are "I understand." As you complete your report, consider that we all know many crimes can be prevented. But people are careless and are unaware about self-protection and safety issues and are overly trustworthy. A purse is stolen at poolside and no one saw anything suspicious, or a suite door was propped open for only five minutes while the victim stepped next door. This is why many hotels place crime and loss prevention literature in the rooms for the guests to read and to be self-educated.

134.

Teamwork

Teamwork is the result of a group of people and departments within your organization who work together to accomplish the same result(s). If teamwork does not exist, the major percentage of your hard labor will be rendered fruitless. Teamwork is:

1. Communication.

2. Shared briefings.

3. Healthy and comfortable working environment.

4. Leaving ego at home.

5. No secrets within your surveillance department unless otherwise ordered by upper management to preserve the integrity of a certain investigation.

6. Clear policies and procedures dictating proper chain of command and the responsibilities of each level. Proper chain of command is very important. Compare chain of command to a linked chain. If a link is broken in that chain, the strength of the chain ends at it weakest link.

7. Trust fellow team members. If you feel a member of your team will throw the game, get rid of that player immediately.

8. Being honest. If you do not know the answer to a question, say "I don't know." It's more beneficial to your team to be honest from the get go than trying to cover any mistake(s) at a later time.

9. Doing your homework. Are you providing everything your team has to offer? Make a checklist of "Things to do" if necessary.

10. Keep good case logs and reports for future reference which your team feels may help protect your company's assets and liabilities in the future.

Section J:
Federal Regulations:
Cash Transactions, Prohibitions,
Reporting, and Record Keeping

135.

6A.010 Definitions. As Used in Regulation 6A:

1.   "Affiliate" has the same meaning as defined in Regulation 15.482–3.

2.   "Branch office" means any person that has been delegated the authority by a nonrestricted licensee to conduct cash transactions on behalf of the nonrestricted licensee. The term does not include any person who is not an affiliate of the nonrestricted licensee and who only has the authority to accept credit repayments. The term also does not include persons who are financial institutions pursuant to 31 C.F.R. Part 103.

3.   "Cash" means coin and currency that circulates, and is customarily used and accepted as money, in the issuing nation.

4.   "Chairman" means the chairman or other member of the state gaming control board.

5.   "Designated 24-hour period" means the 24-hour period designated by a 6A licensee in its system of internal control submitted pursuant to Regulation 6.090.

6.   "Gaming instrumentality" means a wagering instrument or other instrumentality approved by the chairman.

7.   "Nonrestricted licensee" means any person holding a nonrestricted gaming license, an operator of a slot machine route, or an operator of an intercasino linked system, and the principal headquarters or any branch office or other place of business of the nonrestricted licensee.

8.   "Patron" means any person, whether or not engaged in gaming, who enters into a transaction governed by Regulation 6A with a 6A licensee and includes, but is not limited to, officers, employees, and agents of a 6A licensee, but does not include:

   a.   Banks as defined in 31 C.F.R. pt. 103;

   b.   Foreign banks as defined in 31 C.F.R. pt. 103;

    c.   Currency dealers or exchangers as defined in 31 C.F.R. pt. 103;

    d.   Officers, employees, and agents of a 6A licensee conducting internal transactions or transactions with a nonrestricted licensee in the ordinary course of the 6A licensee's operations other than those transactions which directly facilitate or are intended to facilitate gaming activity;

    e.   A nonrestricted licensee conducting a transaction with a 6A licensee arising in the ordinary course of both licensees' operations and where the transaction is not for the benefit of another person; or

    f.   A person or an agent of a person that operates a casino chip and token exchange business when performing chip and token exchanges.

    g.   A person conducting a non-gaming related transaction at a hotel front desk, gift shop, restaurant, box office of other non-gaming area of a 6A licensee's establishment.

9.   "6A licensee" means any person holding a nonrestricted gaming license, its principal headquarters and any branch office or other place of business of the 6A licensee:

    a.   Having annual gross gaming revenue of $10 million or more for the 12 months ending June 30 of each year and having table games statistical win of $2 million or more for the 12 months ending June 30 of each year; or

    b.   Having actual or projected annual gross gaming revenue of $1 million or more for the 12 months ending June 30 that the chairman designates as a 6A licensee for a specific length of time. The chairman's decision shall be considered an administrative decision, and therefore reviewable pursuant to the procedures set forth in Regulations 4.185, 4.190 and 4.195. The chairman shall notify the affected nonrestricted licensee of its designation, in writing, at least 60 days before the nonrestricted licensee would be subject to compliance with Regulation 6A. The chairman may cancel such designations or renew such designations. Once a nonrestricted licensee qualifies as a "6A licensee" pursuant to subsection (a), they shall always be designated as a "6A licensee" in subsequent years unless the chairman cancels such designations in writing pursuant to this subsection (b).

(Adopted: 1/97. Effective: 5/1/97.)

136.

6A.020 Prohibited Transactions; Exceptions

1. A 6A licensee shall not exchange cash for cash with or on behalf of a patron in any transaction in which the amount of the exchange is more than $3,000.

2. A 6A licensee shall not issue a check, other negotiable instrument, or combination thereof, to a patron in exchange for cash in any transaction in which the amount of the exchange is more than $3,000.

3. A 6A licensee shall not effect any transfer of funds by electronic, wire, or other method, or combination of methods, to a patron, or otherwise effect any transfer of funds by any means on behalf of a patron, in exchange for cash in any transaction in which the amount of the exchange is more than $3,000.

4. This section does not restrict a 6A licensee from transferring a patron's funds to the 6A licensee's affiliate if the affiliate complies with subsection 1, 2, or 3 for that transaction.

5. This section does not restrict a 6A licensee from transferring a patron's winnings by check, other negotiable instrument, electronic, wire, or other transfer of funds if the check, negotiable instrument, electronic, wire or other transfer of funds issued by a 6A licensee in payment of a patron's winnings is made payable to the order of the patron and, if the winnings have been paid:

    (a) In cash but the patron has not taken physical possession of the cash or has not removed the cash from the sight of the 6A licensee's employee who paid the winnings; or

    (b) With chips, tokens, or other gaming instrumentalities.

6. This section does not prohibit a 6A licensee from selling coin to, or purchasing coin from, a patron if the 6A licensee completes the identification, recordkeeping and reporting requirements described in Regulation 6A.030 for all exchanges or series of exchanges in excess of $10,000 conducted by an employee of the 6A licensee in any one designated 24-hour period.

7.   This section does not prohibit a 6A licensee from accepting cash from and returning it to a patron in accordance with this subsection. If a patron delivers more than $3,000 in cash to a 6A licensee in any transaction and the 6A licensee has knowledge of the amount delivered, the 6A licensee shall, for each delivery, segregate the cash delivered and return only that cash to the patron, or record the denominations and the number of bills of each denomination of the cash delivered and, for all full and partial returns of each delivery, return to the patron only cash of the same denominations and no more than the same number of bills of each denomination as was delivered, and record the denominations and the number of bills of each denomination of the cash returned. For each delivery, regardless of the method used, the amount delivered may be returned by check, other negotiable instrument, or wire, electronic, or other method of transfer, only if the employee handling the transaction is reasonably assured that the deposited funds were the proceeds of gaming winnings and that the return will not violate subsection 1, 2, or 3.

(Adopted: 1/97. Effective: 5/1/97.)

137.

6A.030 Reportable Transactions

1.   Except as otherwise provided in Regulation 6A, a 6A licensee shall report each of the following:

    a.   Cash-in transactions where an employee of the 6A licensee accepts or receives more than $10,000 in cash from a patron in any transaction:

        1)   As any table game wager where the patron loses the wager;

        2)   As any wager which is not a table game wager;

        3)   In any exchange for its chips, tokens, or other gaming instrumentalities;

        4)   As a repayment of credit previously extended;

        5)   As a deposit for gaming or safekeeping purposes, including a deposit to a race/sports book account, if the 6A licensee has actual knowledge of the amount of cash deposited; or

        6)   Not specifically covered by this paragraph (a).

    b.   Cash-out transactions where an employee of the 6A licensee disburses more than $10,000 in cash to a patron in any transaction:

        1)   As a redemption of chips, tokens, or other gaming instrumentalities;

        2)   As a payment of winning wager(s);

        3)   As a payment of tournament or contest winnings or a promotional payout;

        4)   As a withdrawal of a deposit for gaming or safekeeping purposes, including a withdrawal from a race/sports book account, if the 6A licensee has actual knowledge of the amount of cash withdrawn;

        5)   In exchange for a check or other negotiable instrument;

        6)   In exchange for an electronic, wire or other transfer of funds;

    7) As a credit advance (including markers);

    8) For travel expenses or other complimentary expenses or for a distribution of a gaming incentive such as settlement of a gaming debt, front money discount, or other similar distribution based upon gaming activity;

    9) Not specifically covered by this paragraph (b).

2.   Before completing a transaction for which a report is required under subsection 1, unless the patron is a known patron, a 6A licensee shall:

    a.   Obtain the patron's name;

    b.   Obtain or reasonably attempt to obtain the patron's permanent address and social security or employer identification number;

    c.   Obtain one of the following identification credentials from the patron:

        1) Driver's license;

        2) Passport;

        3) Non-resident alien identification card;

        4) Other reliable government issue identification credential; or

        5) Other picture identification credential normally acceptable as a means of identification when cashing checks; and

    d.   Examine the identification credential obtained, to verify the patron's name, and to the extent possible, to verify the accuracy of the information obtained pursuant to paragraph (b).

        1)   If a person performs a reportable transaction on behalf of a patron, obtain the information and perform the procedures required under paragraphs (a) through (d) with respect to the person performing the transaction.

3.   For each transaction that is reportable pursuant to this section, the 6A licensee shall complete a report that includes:

    a.   The date and the time of the transaction;

b. The dollar amount or, for foreign currency, the United States dollar equivalent of the transaction;

c. The type of transaction, including a designation that:

   1) The report is of multiple transactions pursuant to paragraph (a) of subsection (2) of Regulation 6A.040, if applicable;

   2) The report is of more than one transaction type because the transaction is a multiple dissimilar transaction under paragraphs (b) or (c) of subsection (2) of Regulation 6A.040, if applicable;

   3) A designation that the report is for an additional transaction described in subsection (4) of Regulation 6A.040, if applicable;

d. The patron's name;

e. The patron's permanent address (or post office box number but only if the patron refuses to provide a permanent address);

f. The type, number and issuing entity of the identification credential presented by the patron;

g. The patron's social security or employer identification number;

h. The patron's date of birth, if so indicated on the patron's identification credential or if contained in the 6A licensee's records;

i. The patron's account number with the 6A licensee, if applicable, as related to the transaction being reported;

j. The method used to verify the patron's identity and permanent address;

k. The signature of the person handling the transaction and recording the information on behalf of the 6A licensee;

l. The signature of a person other than the person who handled the transaction reviewing the report of behalf of the 6A licensee;

m. The reason any item in paragraphs (a) through (l) is not documented on the report; and

n. The 6A licensee's name and the business address where the transaction took place.

4. If a person performs the transaction on behalf of a patron, the licensee shall obtain and report the information required by paragraphs (a) through (j) of subsection 3 with respect to the person performing the transaction, and the 6A licensee shall reasonably attempt to obtain and, to the extent obtained, shall report the information required by paragraphs (a) through (j) of subsection 3 with respect to the patron;

5. If a patron tenders more than $10,000 in chips, tokens, or gaming instrumentalities to a 6A licensee for cash redemption, or is to be paid more than $10,000 in cash for a slot, bingo, keno, race, sports, or any other gaming win, but is unable to obtain the patron's name and identification credential, the 6A licensee shall not complete the transaction. If the 6A licensee and the patron are unable to resolve the dispute regarding payment of alleged winnings to the patron's satisfaction, the 6A licensee shall immediately notify the board, and the matter shall thereafter proceed pursuant to NRS 463.362, 463.363, 463.364, and 463.366.

6. If a patron attempts to place a cash wager of more than $10,000 at any table game, the 6A licensee shall complete the identification and recordkeeping requirements of subsection 2 before accepting the wager.

7. If a 6A licensee discovers it has completed a transaction without complying with subsection 2, the 6A licensee shall attempt to obtain the necessary information and identification credential from the patron. If the patron refuses to provide or is unavailable to provide the necessary information and identification credentials, the 6A licensee shall bar the patron from gaming at the 6A licensee's establishment and at the establishments of the 6A licensee's affiliates until the patron supplies the necessary information and identification credential. The 6A licensee shall inform the patron that the patron is barred from gaming at the 6A licensee's establishment and at the establishments of the 6A licensee's affiliates if the patron is at the 6A licensee's establishment or at one of its affiliates. If the patron refuses to provide identification credentials or is unavailable for identification purposes, the 6A licensee shall complete a report pursuant to this section to the extent possible.

8. As used in this section, a "known patron" means a patron known to the 6A licensee's employee handling the transaction with the patron, for whom the 6A licensee has previously obtained the patron's name and identification credential, and with respect to whom the 6A licensee has on file and periodically, as required in Regulation 6.090 minimum standards for internal control, updates all the information needed to complete a report. Reports of transactions with known patrons shall indicate on the report "known patron, information on file" as the method of verification and shall include the original method of identification, including type and number, of the identification credential originally examined.

9.   **[Effective until 11/1/97]** Each licensee shall report the information required to be reported under this section on a Currency Transaction Report by Casinos, Nevada (CTRC–N), a form published by the United States Department of the Treasury, and otherwise in such manner as the chairman may approve or require. Each 6A licensee shall file each report with the United States Internal Revenue Service and a copy thereof with the board no later than 15 days after the occurrence of the recorded transaction. The 6A licensee shall file an amended report if the 6A licensee obtains information to correct or complete a previously submitted report. The amended report shall reference the previously submitted report. Each 6A licensee shall retain a copy of each report filed for at least 5 years unless the chairman requires retention for a longer period of time.

9.   **[Effective 11/1/97]** Each licensee shall report the information required to be reported under this section on a Currency Transaction Report by Casinos, Nevada (CTRC–N), a form published by the United States Department of the Treasury, and otherwise in such manner as the chairman may approve or require. Each 6A licensee shall file each report with the United States Internal Revenue Service no later than 15 days after the occurrence of the recorded transaction. The 6A licensee shall file an amended report if the 6A licensee obtains information to correct or complete a previously submitted report. The amended report shall reference the previously submitted report. Each 6A licensee shall retain a copy of each report filed for at least 5 years unless the chairman requires retention for a longer period of time.

(Adopted: 1/97. Effective: 5/1/97, except (9) as noted.)

138.

6A.040 Multiple Transactions

1. A 6A licensee and its employees and agents shall not knowingly allow, and each 6A licensee shall take reasonable steps to prevent, the circumvention of Regulation 6A.020 and 6A.030 by multiple transactions within its designated 24-hour period with a patron or a patron's agent or by the use of a series of transactions that are designed to accomplish indirectly that which could not be accomplished directly. As part of a 6A licensee's efforts to prevent such circumventions relative to Regulation 6A.030, a 6A licensee shall establish and implement multiple transaction logs pursuant to Regulation 6.090 minimum standards for internal control.

2. Each 6A licensee shall aggregate transactions in excess of $3,000, or in smaller amounts when any single officer, employee, or agent of the 6A licensee has actual knowledge of the transactions or would in the ordinary course of business have reason to know of the transactions between the 6A licensee and a patron or a person who the 6A licensee knows or has reason to know is the patron's confederate or agent. The 6A licensee shall aggregate:

   a. During a designated 24-hour period, the same type transactions occurring within each of the following areas:

      1) At a single specific cage;

      2) At a single specific gaming pit (which is a series or group of gaming tables under the supervision of a single floor supervisor); or

      3) At another single specific gaming or other monitoring area as described in the 6A licensee's system of internal controls submitted pursuant to Regulation 6.090; or

   b. During a designated 24-hour period, transactions in which the 6A licensee receives cash from the patron during a single visit to one gaming table, one single slot machine, or one single cage window, race book window, sports book window, keno window, bingo window, slot booth window or branch office; or

   c. During a designated 24-hour period, transactions in which the 6A licensee disburses cash to the patron during a single visit to one single gaming table, one single slot machine, or one single cage window, race book window, sports book window, keno window, bingo window, slot booth window or branch office.

3. Before completing a transaction that, when aggregated with others pursuant to subsection 2, will aggregate to an amount that will exceed $10,000, the 6A licensee shall complete the identification and recordkeeping requirements described in subsection (2) of Regulation 6A.030. When aggregated transactions exceed $10,000, the 6A licensee shall complete the reporting requirements of Regulation 6A.030.

4. If a patron performs a transaction that pursuant to paragraph (a) of subsection 2 is to be aggregated with previous transactions for which a report has been completed pursuant to this section or Regulation 6A.030, the 6A licensee shall complete the identification and reporting procedures described in Regulation 6A.030 for the additional transaction, provided that only one report need be completed for all such additional transactions by the patron during a designated 24-hour period, and provided further that all such additional transactions shall be reported regardless of amount.

5. As used in this section:

   a. "Single visit" means one single, continuous appearance at a given location uninterrupted by a patron's physical absence from that given location during a designated 24-hour period.

   b. "Same type transactions" means transactions in any one and only one of the transaction categories delineated in Regulation 6A.030(1).

(Adopted: 1/97. Effective: 5/1/97.)

139.

6A.050 Record Keeping Requirements

Each 6A licensee, in such manner as the chairman or his designee may approve or require, shall create and keep accurate, complete, legible, and permanent original (unless otherwise specified in Regulation 6A and Regulation 6.090 minimum standards relative to Regulation 6A) records to ensure compliance with Regulation 6A within Nevada for a period of five years unless the chairman approves or requires otherwise in writing. Each 6A licensee shall provide the audit division, upon its request, the records required to be maintained by Regulation 6A. These records shall include:

1. For transactions involving more than $3,000 with respect to each deposit of funds, including gaming front money deposits or safekeeping deposits, account opened, or line of credit extended or established, 6A licensees shall, at the time the funds are deposited, the account is opened, or credit is extended or established, secure and maintain the same information as required in Regulations 6A.030(3)(d) through (j) in the manner required in Regulation 6A.030(1). Where the deposit, account, or credit is in the names of two or more patrons, the 6A licensee shall secure such information for each patron having a financial interest in the deposit, account, or line of credit. In the event a 6A licensee has been unable to secure all the required information, it shall not be deemed to be in violation of this section if it has made a reasonable effort to secure such information, maintains a list containing the names and permanent addresses of those patrons from whom it has been unable to obtain the information, and makes the names and addresses of those patrons available to the state upon request.

2. Either the original or a microfilm or other copy or reproduction of each of the following:

    a. A record of each receipt of more than $3,000 (including but not limited to funds for safekeeping or front money) of funds received by the 6A licensee for the account (credit or deposit) of any patron. The record shall include the same information required in Regulation 6A.030(3)(d) through (j) for a patron from whom the funds were received, as well as the date and amount of the funds received. If the patron from whom the funds were received indicates and the 6A licensee has reason to believe that the patron is a nonresident alien, the 6A licensee shall obtain and record the patron's passport number and country of issue, or a description of some other government document used to verify the patron's identity.

b. Each statement, ledger card, or other record of each deposit account or credit account with the 6A licensee, showing each transaction (including deposits, receipts, withdrawals, disbursements, or transfers) in, or with respect to, a patron's deposit account or credit account with the 6A licensee.

c. A record of each bookkeeeping entry (e.g., source document or other posting media) recording a debit or credit to a patron's deposit account or credit account with the 6A licensee.

d. A record of each extension of credit in excess of $3,000, the terms and conditions of the extension of credit, and repayments. The record shall be included in the information required in paragraphs (a) and (b) and the date and amount of each transaction.

e. In instances in which the following transactions are not prohibited, a record of each advice, request, or instruction:

    1) Received or given regarding any transaction resulting (or intended to result and later canceled if such a record is normally made) in the transfer of funds, or of currency, other monetary instruments, funds, checks, investment securities, or credit, of more than $3,000 to or from any person, account, or place outside the United States.

    2) Given to another financial institution or other person located within or without the United States, regarding a transaction intended to result in the transfer of funds, or of currency, other monetary instruments, checks, investment securities, or credit, of more than $3,000 to a person, account, or place outside the United States.

f. To the extent relevant to any matter relating to the enforcement of Regulation 6A, records prepared or received by the 6A licensee in the ordinary course of business that would be needed:

    1) To reconstruct a patron's deposit account or credit account with the 6A licensee in a manner that is in accordance with Regulation 6.090 minimum standards for internal control;

2) To trace a check or other negotiable instrument tendered with the 6A licensee through the 6A licensee's records to the bank of deposit in a manner that is in accordance with Regulation 6.090 minimum standards for internal control; or

3) To trace a check, negotiable instrument, or other transfer of funds tendered in exchange for a 6A licensee's check, negotiable instrument or other transfer of funds through the 6A licensee's records to the bank of deposit in a manner that is in accordance with Regulation 6.090 minimum standards for internal control.

g. Player rating records, or summaries that summarize player rating records in accordance with Regulation 6.090 minimum standards for internal control, if the records or summaries are:

1) Prepared as a source document to reflect cash activity and used for purposes of complying with Regulation 6A; or

2) Used to substantiate a Suspicious Activity Report by Casinos which is based in whole or part on the transactions recorded on the rating record. Both original and summary records should be retained in this situation, if possible.

3. To the extent relevant to any matter relating to the enforcement of Regulation 6A, all records, documents, or manuals required to be maintained by a 6A licensee under state and local laws or regulations.

4. Any records required either by Regulation 6.090 minimum standards for internal control relative to Regulation 6A or by the 6A licensee's system of internal control relative to Regulation 6A. Each 6A licensee shall also maintain records of the 6A licensee's steps to implement policies and procedures that are designed to meet the 6A licensee's responsibilities under these requirements (e.g., internal procedures and instructions to employees, records of internal audits).

5. Any additional records the chairman, the board, or the commission require any 6A licensee to make and maintain to insure compliance with Regulation 6A.

(Adopted: 1/97. Effective: 5/1/97.)

140.

6A.060 Internal Control

1. Each 6A licensee shall include as part of its system of internal control submitted pursuant to Regulation 6.090 a description of the procedures adopted by the 6A licensee to comply with this Regulation. Each 6A licensee shall comply with both its system of internal control and the Regulation 6.090 minimum standards for internal control relative to Regulation 6A.

2. Each 6A licensee shall direct an independent accountant engaged by the 6A licensee to report at least annually to the 6A licensee and to the board regarding the 6A licensee's adherence to the provisions of Regulation 6A and regarding the effectiveness and adequacy of the form and operation of the 6A licensee's systems of internal control as they relate to the provisions of Regulation 6A. Using criteria established by the chairman, the independent accountant shall report each event and procedures discovered by or brought to the attention of the independent accountant that the accountant believes do not conform with Regulation 6A, with Regulation 6.090 minimum standards for internal control relative to Regulation 6A or any approved variation pursuant to subsection 6, or with the 6A licensee's system of internal control as they relate to Regulation 6A, regardless of the materiality or nonmateriality of the exceptions. Such reports shall be submitted to the board within 150 days of the 6A licensee's fiscal year end and shall be accompanied by the 6A licensee's statement addressing each item of noncompliance noted by the accountant and describing the action taken.

3. The chairman may waive any of the requirements in subsection 2 at his discretion.

4. Each 6A licensee shall establish and maintain a compliance program pursuant to Regulation 6.090 minimum standards for internal control and shall at all times provide for an individual as a compliance specialist for the 6A licensee. The compliance specialist shall be responsible for assuring day-to-day regulatory compliance for the 6A licensee, relative to Regulation 6A and Regulation 6.090 minimum standards for internal control for Regulation 6A.

5. Each 6A licensee shall establish and maintain a training program pursuant

to Regulation 6.090 minimum standards for internal control.

6. The 6A licensee shall implement a system of internal control that satisfies the minimum standards relative to Regulation 6A unless the chairman, in his sole discretion, determines that the 6A licensee's proposed system satisfies the requirements of Regulation 6A although it does not fully satisfy the minimum standards and approves the variation in writing. Within 30 days after a 6A licensee receives notice of the chairman's approval, the 6A licensee shall comply with the approved procedures, amend its written system accordingly, and submit to the board a copy of the amendments to the written system and a written description of the variations.

(Adopted: 1/97. Effective: 5/1/97.)

141.

6A.070 Construction

Regulation 6A shall be liberally construed and applied in favor of strict regulation of the cash transactions described in Regulation 6A, and in favor of the policies enunciated in the Nevada Gaming Control Act and the regulations of the Nevada gaming commission. Without limiting the generality of the foregoing, substance shall prevail over form and prohibitions of the direct performance of specified acts shall be construed to prohibit indirect performance of those acts.

(Adopted: 1/97. Effective: 5/1/97.)

142.

6A.080 Funds Transfer Requirements

For purposes of this section, each 6A licensee is also a financial institution as described in 31 C.F.R. pt. 103. This section applies to transmittals of funds in an amount that exceeds $3,000.

1. For each transmittal order that it accepts as a transmittor's financial institution, a 6A licensee shall obtain and retain either the original or a microfilm, other copy, or electronic record of the following information relating to the transmittal order:

    a. The name and address of the transmittor;

    b. The amount of the transmittal order;

    c. The execution date of the transmittal order;

    d. Any payment instructions received from the transmittor with the transmittal order;

    e. The identity of the recipient's financial institution;

    f. As many of the following items as are received with the transmittal order:

        1) The name and address of the recipient;

        2) The account number of the recipient; and

        3) Any other specific identifier of the recipient; and

    g. Any form relating to the transmittal of funds that is completed or signed by the person placing the transmittal order.

2. For each transmittal order that it accepts as an intermediary financial institution, a 6A licensee shall retain either the original or a microfilm, other copy, or electronic record of the transmittal order.

3. For each transmittal order that it accepts as a recipient's financial institution, a 6A licensee shall retain either the original or a microfilm, other copy, or electronic record of the transmittal order.

4. For transmittal orders accepted by the 6A licensee as the transmittor's financial institution:

    a. If the transmittal order is made in person, prior to acceptance of a transmittal order the 6A licensee shall verify the identity of the person placing the transmittal order in the same manner as required in Regulation 6A.030(2). If it accepts the transmittal order, the 6A licensee shall obtain and retain a record of the information required in Regulation 6A.030(3)(d) through (j). Where an agent is involved in the transaction and information regarding a principal of a transaction is not available, a notation in the record to that extent shall be made.

    b. If the transmittal order accepted by the 6A licensee is not made in person, the 6A licensee shall obtain and retain a record of the information required in Regulation 6A.030(3)(d) through (j). Where an agent is involved in the transaction and information regarding a principal of a transaction is not available, a notation in the record to that extent shall be made.

5. For each transmittal order that the 6A licensee accepts as a recipient's financial institution for a recipient, obtain and retain either the original or a microfilm, other copy, or electronic record of the transmittal order:

    a. If the proceeds are delivered in person to the recipient or its agent, the 6A licensee shall verify the identity of the person receiving the proceeds in the same manner as Regulation 6A.030(2) and shall obtain and retain a record of the information required in Regulation 6A.030(3)(d) through (j). Where an agent is involved in the transaction and information regarding a principal of a transaction is not available, a notation in the record to that extent shall be made.

    b. If the proceeds are delivered other than in person, the 6A licensee shall retain a copy of the check or other instrument used to effect payment, or the information contained thereon, as well as the name and address of the person to which it was sent.

6. Any 6A licensee as transmittor's financial institution or as an intermediary financial institution shall include in any transmittal order the following information:

     a. As transmittor's financial institution at the time the transmittal order is sent to a receiving financial institution, the following information:

       1) The name and, if the payment is ordered from an account, the account number of the transmittor;

       2) The address of the transmittor;

       3) The amount of the transmittal order;

       4) The execution date of the transmittal order;

       5) The identity of the recipient's financial institution;

       6) As many of the following items as are received with the transmittal order:

7.   The name and address of the recipient;

     a. The account number of the recipient;

     b. Any other specific identifier of the recipient; and

       1) Either the name and address or numerical identifier of the transmittor's financial institution.

8.   As an intermediary financial institution, if it accepts a transmittal order, in a corresponding transmittal order at the time it is sent to the next receiving financial institution, the following information, if received from the sender:

     a. The name and account number of the transmittor;

     b. The address of the transmittor;

     c. The amount of the transmittal order;

     d. The execution date of the transmittal order;

     e. The identity of the recipient's financial institution;

     f. As many of the following items as are received with the transmittal order:

       1) The name and address of the recipient;

       2) The account number of the recipient;

3) Any other specific identifier of the recipient; and

g. Either the name and address or numerical identifier of the transmittor's financial institution.

9. A 6A licensee:

a. As a transmittor's financial institution will be deemed to be in compliance with the provisions of paragraph (a) of subsection 6 if it:

1) Includes in the transmittal order, at the time it is sent to the receiving financial institution, the information specified in paragraph (a) of subsection 6 to the extent that such information has been received by the 6A licensee; and

2) Provides the information specified in paragraph (a) of subsection 6 to a financial institution that acted as an intermediary financial institution or recipient's financial institution in connection with the transmittal order, within a reasonable time after any such financial institution makes a request therefor in connection with the requesting financial institution's receipt of a lawful request for such information from a federal, state, or local law enforcement or financial regulatory agency, or in connection with the requesting financial institution's own Regulation 6A or United States Title 31 compliance program.

b. As an intermediary financial institution will be deemed to be in compliance with the provisions of paragraph (b) of subsection 6 if it:

1) Includes in the transmittal order, at the time it is sent to the receiving financial institution, the information specified in paragraph (b) of subsection 6, to the extent that such information has been received by the 6A licensee; and

2) Provides the information specified in paragraph (b) of subsection 6, to the extent that such information has been received by the 6A licensee, to a financial institution that acted as an intermediary financial institution or recipient's financial institution in connection with the transmittal order, within a reasonable time after any such financial institution makes a request therefor in connection with the requesting financial institution's receipt of a lawful request for such information from a federal, state, or local law

enforcement or regulatory agency, or in connection with the requesting financial institution's own Regulation 6A or United States Title 31 compliance program.

c. Shall treat any information requested under subparagraph (2) of paragraph (a) and under subparagraph (2) of paragraph (b), once received, as if it had been included in the transmittal order to which such information relates.

10. The information that a 6A licensee shall retain as the transmittor's financial institution shall be retrievable by reference to the name of the transmittor and account number, if applicable. The information that a 6A licensee shall retain as a recipient's financial institution shall be retrievable by reference to the name of the recipient and account number, if applicable. This information need not be retained in any particular manner, so long as the 6A licensee is able to retrieve the information required by this section, either by accessing transmittal of funds records directly or through reference to some other record maintained by the 6A licensee.

11. The following transmittals of funds are not subject to the requirements of this section where the transmittor and the recipient of the same transmittal are any of the following:

a. A bank;

b. A wholly-owned domestic subsidiary of a bank chartered in the United States;

c. A broker or dealer in securities;

d. A wholly-owned domestic subsidiary of a broker or dealer in securities;

e. The United States;

f. A state or local government; or

g. A federal, state or local government agency or instrumentality.

12. As used in this section:

a. "Financial institution" means a financial institution as described in 31 C.F.R. pt. 103.

b. "Foreign financial agency" means a foreign financial agency as described in 31 C.F.R. pt. 103.

c. "Receiving financial institution" means the financial institution or foreign financial agency to which the sender's instruction is addressed. The term "receiving financial institution" includes a receiving bank.

d. "Recipient's financial institution" means the financial institution or foreign financial agency identified in a transmittal order in which an account of the recipient is to be credited pursuant to the transmittal order or which otherwise is to make payment to the recipient if the order does not provide for payment to an account. The term "recipient's financial institution" includes a beneficiary's bank, except where the beneficiary is a recipient's financial institution.

e. "Transmittor" means the sender of the first transmittal order in a transmittal of funds. The term "transmittor" includes an originator, except where the transmittor's financial institution is a financial institution or foreign financial agency other than a bank or foreign bank.

f. "Transmittor's financial institution" means the receiving financial institution to which the transmittal order of the transmittor is issued if the transmittor is not a financial institution or a foreign financial agency, or the transmittor if the transmittor is a financial institution or a foreign financial agency. The term "transmittor's financial institution" includes an originator's bank, except where the originator is a transmittor's financial institution other than a bank or foreign bank.

g. "Transmittal order" means an instruction of a sender, including a payment order, to a receiving financial institution, transmitted orally, electronically, or in writing, to pay, or cause another financial institution or foreign financial agency to pay, a fixed or determinable amount of money to a recipient if:

    1) The instruction does not state a condition to payment to the recipient other than time of payment;

    2) The receiving financial institution is to be reimbursed by debiting an account of, or otherwise receiving payment from, the sender; and

    3) The instruction is transmitted by the sender directly to the receiving financial institution or to an agent or communication system for transmittal to the receiving financial institution.

(Adopted: 1/97. Effective: 5/1/97.)

143.

6A.090 Structured Transactions

1. A 6A licensee, its officers, employees or agents shall not encourage or instruct the patron to structure or attempt to structure transactions. This subsection does not prohibit a 6A licensee from informing a patron of the regulatory requirements imposed upon the 6A licensee, including the definition of structured transactions.

2. A 6A licensee, its officers, employees or agents shall not knowingly assist a patron in structuring or in attempting to structure transactions.

3. As used in this section, "structure transactions" or "structuring transactions" means to willfully conduct or attempt to conduct a series of cash or noncash transactions in any amount, at one or more 6A licensees, on one or more days in any manner as to willfully evade or circumvent the reporting requirements of Regulation 6A.030 or in such a manner as to willfully evade the prohibitions of Regulation 6A.020. The transaction or transactions need not exceed the dollar thresholds in Regulation 6A.020 and Regulation 6A.030 at any single 6A licensee in any single day in order to constitute structuring within the meaning of this definition.

(Adopted: 1/97. Effective: 5/1/97.)

144.

6A.100 Suspicious Activity Reports

As used in this section:

1. "Suspicious transaction" means a transaction conducted or attempted by, at, or through the 6A licensee that the 6A licensee knows or, in the judgment of the 6A licensee or its officers, employees and agents, has reason to suspect:

2. Involves funds derived from illegal activities or is conducted or intended to be conducted to hide or disguise funds or assets derived from illegal activities (including, without limitation, the ownership, nature, source, location, or control of such funds or assets) as part of a plan to violate or evade any federal or state law or regulation or to avoid any transaction reporting requirement under federal or state law or regulation;

3. Is designed to willfully evade any requirements of Regulation 6A including the structuring of transactions or attempting to structure transactions; or

4. Has no business or apparent lawful purpose or is not the sort of transaction in which the particular patron would normally be expected to engage, and the 6A licensee knows of no reasonable explanation for the transaction after examining the available facts, including the background and possible purpose of the transaction.

5. "Transaction" means a purchase, sale, loan, pledge, gift, transfer, delivery, or other disposition, and, with respect to a financial institution or 6A licensee, includes a deposit, withdrawal, transfer between accounts, exchange of currency, loan, extension of credit, purchase or sale of any stock, bond, certificate of deposit, casino chips, tokens, or other gaming instrumentalities or other investment security or monetary instrument, or any other payment, transfer, or delivery by, through, or to a financial institution or 6A licensee, by whatever means effected.

6. A 6A licensee:

    a. Shall file with FinCEN, by using the SARC specified in subsection 3, a report of any suspicious transaction, if it involves or aggregates to more than $3,000 in funds or other assets;

b. May file with FinCEN, by using the SARC specified in subsection 3, a report of any suspicious transaction, regardless of the amount, that the 6A licensee believes is relevant to the possible violation of any law or regulation but whose reporting is not required by this section;

7. A suspicious transaction shall be reported by completing a SARC, and collecting and maintaining supporting documentation as required by subsection 5. The SARC:

a. Shall be filed with FinCEN in a central location, to be determined by FinCEN and with a copy sent to the board as indicated in the instructions to the SARC; and

b. Shall be filed no later than 30 calendar days after the initial detection by the 6A licensee of facts that may constitute a basis for filing a SARC. If no suspect was identified on the date of the detection of the incident requiring the filing, a 6A licensee may delay filing a SARC for an additional 30 calendar days to identify a suspect. In no case shall reporting be delayed more than 60 calendar days after the date of initial detection of a reportable transaction. In situations involving violations that require immediate attention, such as, for example, ongoing money laundering schemes, the 6A licensee shall immediately notify, by telephone, an appropriate law enforcement authority in addition to filing timely a SARC.

8. A 6A licensee is not required to file a SARC for a robbery or burglary committed or attempted or for lost, missing, counterfeit, or stolen securities, that is reported to appropriate law enforcement authorities.

9. A 6A licensee shall maintain a copy of any SARC filed and the original or business record equivalent of any supporting documentation for a period of five years from the date of filing the SARC. Supporting documentation shall be identified, and maintained by the 6A licensee as such, and shall be deemed to have been filed with the SARC. A 6A licensee shall make all supporting documentation available to FinCEN and the board and any appropriate law enforcement agencies upon request.

10. No 6A licensee and no director, officer, employee, or agent of any 6A licensee or other financial institution, who reports a suspicious transac-

tion under this part, shall notify any person involved in the transaction that the transaction has been reported. The copy of any such SARC filed with the board is privileged under NRS 463.3407 and may be disclosed only to the board and the commission in the necessary administration of Regulation 6A. A 6A licensee has protection pursuant to Nevada Revised Statutes and to 31 U.S.C. 5318(g) regarding a SARC filed pursuant to this section.

11. As used in this section:

    a. "FinCEN" means the Financial Crimes Enforcement Network, an office within the Office of the Under Secretary (Enforcement) of the United States Department of the Treasury.

    b. "SARC" means Suspicious Activity Report by Casinos, a form published by the United States Department of the Treasury.

(Adopted: 1/97. Effective: 10/1/97.)

145.

6A.110 Waivers

The chairman may approve the conduct of a particular transaction or type of transaction with a specific patron that would otherwise be prohibited under Regulation 6A.020 and may waive the reporting of a particular transaction or type of transaction with a specific patron for which a report would otherwise be required under Regulation 6A.030. Requests for such approvals and waivers shall be made in advance of the transaction and be evidenced in writing to the chairman. The chairman may grant or deny such requests and revoke approvals and waivers previously granted.

(Adopted: 1/97. Effective: 5/1/97.)

146.

Suspicious Activity Report by Casinos (SARC)

1. Definition

   "Suspicious transaction" means a transaction conducted or attempted by, at, or through the 6A licensee that, the 6A licensee knows or, in the judgment of the 6A licensee or its officers, employees and agents, has reason to suspect;

2. The transaction involves funds derived from illegal activities;

3. The transaction is designed to willfully evade any requirements of Regulation 6A including structuring; or

4. The transaction has no apparent business or logical purpose for the transaction.

5. Filing

   Suspicious Activity is to be documented on form TD F 90-22.49 Suspicious Activity Report by Casinos ('SARC") promulgated by the Financial Crimes Enforcement Network ("FinCEN"). This form is designed for both Nevada 6A Licensees and Title 31 Licensees.

   The form implies regulatory standards, which are at odds with Regulation 6A.100, which is the regulation that requires Nevada 6A Licensees to report suspicious transactions.

   For suspicious transactions, a SARC is completed within 24-hours once the transaction is considered suspicious. The SARC is forwarded to the accounting department within 24-hours of the completion of the form.

   The following points and instructions are to clarify these items (as advised by outside legal counsel).

6. Points

       Suspicious Activity Reports by Casinos (SARC):

    a. Are filed for suspicious transactions if it involves or aggregates to more than $3,000 in funds or assets.

    b. May be filed for suspicious transaction(s) regardless of the amount if the 6A licensee believes it is relevant to the possible violation of any law but whose reporting is not required by this section.

    c. Shall be filed with the FinCEN, a section of the U.S. Department of Treasury, within 30 (thirty) days after initial detection of suspicious activity. A copy shall also be filed with the Gaming Control Board.

    d. The law prohibits informing any person included in the transaction that a SARC is being filed for suspicious transactions under any circumstances.

    e. There is no affirmative duty to investigate or research the information requested in Part II –Suspect Information- of the SARC. If the requested information in part II is not known by the preparer and/or witness (if applicable), then "unknown" should be documented in the applicable boxes in part II.

    f. A description of the suspect is not required in the instructions on completing the form. Therefore, the suspect's description information known by the preparer and/or witness needs only to be used, at the discretion of the preparer, in the narrative explanation.

Suspicious Activity Information–Narrative Explanation/Description

Explanation/Description of known or Suspected Violation of Law(s) or Suspicious Activity. Provide a clear and concise account of the possible violation of law(s). Describe in detail what is unusual, irregular or suspicious about the activity. Use the checklist below as you prepare your account. This section of the report is critical. The care with which it is written may make the difference in whether or not the described suspicious conduct and/or its possible criminal nature are clearly understood.

1.   Provide a brief chronological summary of the suspicious activity.

2.   Indicate where the possible violation of law(s) took place (e.g., branch, cage, specific gaming pit, specific gaming areas, etc.).

3. Explain who benefited, financially or otherwise from the transaction(s). how much and how; whether completed or only attempted.

4. Describe suspects' position if a casino employee (e.g., dealer, pit supervisor, cage cashier, host, director of marketing, etc.).

5. Indicate whether funds or assets were recovered and, if so, enter the dollar value of the recovery in whole dollars only.

6. Indicate whether the possible violation of law(s) is an isolated incident or relates to another transaction(s).

7. Indicate whether there is any other related litigation; if so, specify its status.

8. Describe supporting documentation, including any video or audio tapes and credit bureau report which relate to the activity.

9. Describe any additional information which is necessary to fully understand the unusual, irregular or suspicious nature of the activity.

10. Recommend any further investigation that might assist law enforcement authorities.

For Money Laundering, Structuring, or Wire Transfer referrals, please include the following additional information:

11. Indicate whether U.S. or foreign currency and/or monetary instrument(s) were involved. If so, provide the amount and/or description.

12. Indicate any additional casino account number(s) and any domestic or foreign bank(s) and/or account number(s) which may be involved.

13. Indicate for a foreign national any available information on U.S. or foreign visas including country and/or city of issuance, or temporary U.S. address.

Retain for a Period of Five Years:

a. All supporting documentation, including any video or audio tapes and credit bureau report which relate to the suspicious activity.

b. Any confession, admission, or explanation of the transaction(s) provided by the suspect(s) and indicate to whom and when it was given.

c. Any confession, admission, explanation or interview concerning the transaction(s) provided by any other person(s) and indicate to whom and when it was given.

d. Any evidence of cover-up or evidence of an attempt to deceive federal or state gaming regulators or others.

All supporting documentation must be made available, upon request, to appropriate law enforcement authorities and regulatory agencies.

147.

Witness Information (if applicable)

Witness's name. If there was a witness to the suspicious activity, enter that person's name in items 44 through 46. This witness may or may not be an employee of the casino. If there is more than one witness (i.e., a group of witnesses or several addresses). Also, complete and write the casino's legal name, casino's trade name, and EIN.

Title/Occupation. If the witness is a casino employee, enter the witness's job title. If not, enter the witness's occupation or business.

Permanent address. Enter the witness's permanent street address, city, two-letter state abbreviation, and ZIP code. Also, enter any apartment number of suite number and road or route number. Do not enter a P.O. box number unless the witness has no street address. If the individual is from a foreign country, enter any province name and the appropriate two-letter country code.

Date of Birth. Enter the witness's date of birth.

Residence phone number. Enter the witness's residence telephone number including area code.

Work phone number. Enter the witness's work telephone number including area code.

Was witness interviewed by casino or a law enforcement agency? Check box a if the witness was interviewed by personnel of the casino or a law enforcement agency. Enter the name of the individual who interviewed the witness, the interviewers organization name, and summarize the substantive information from the interview in Part VIII. If no witness was interviewed, check box b.

Preparer Information
Preparer's name. Enter the person's name who prepared this SARC.
Title. Enter the prepare's job title.
Work phone number. Enter the preparer's work telephone number including area code.
Date prepared. Enter the date prepared. Refer to the instructions for item 29 for proper date format.

Contact Information
Contact's name. Enter the name of the contact.
Title. Enter the contact person's job title.
Work phone number. Enter the contact work telephone number including area code.
Organization name. If the contact person is employed by an organization other than the reporting casino, enter the name of the organization.

148.

Counterfeit*

NRS 465.080 Use of counterfeit, unapproved or unlawful wagering instruments; possession of certain unlawful devices, equipment, products or materials.

1. It is unlawful for any licensee, employee or other person to use counterfeit chips, counterfeit debit instruments or other counterfeit wagering instruments in a gambling game, associated equipment or cashless wagering system.

2. It is unlawful for any person, in playing or using any gambling game, associated equipment or cashless wagering system designed to be played with, receive or be operated by chips, tokens, wagering credits or other wagering instruments approved by the state gaming control board or by lawful coin of the United States of America.

    a. Knowingly to use other than chips, tokens, wagering credits or other wagering instruments approved by the state gaming control board or lawful coin, legal tender of the United States of America, or to use coin or tokens not of the same denomination as the coin or tokens intended to be used in that gambling game, associated equipment or cashless wagering system; or

    b. To use any device or means to violate the provisions of this chapter.

3. It is unlawful for any person, not a duly authorized employee of a licensee acting in furtherance of his employment within an establishment, to have on his person or in his possession on or off the premises of any licensed gaming establishment any device intended to be used to violate the provisions of this chapter.

4. It is unlawful for any person, not a duly authorized employee of a licensee acting in furtherance of his employment within an establishment, to have on his person or in his possession on or off the premises of any licensed gaming establishment any key or device known to have been designed for the purpose of and suitable for opening, entering or affecting the operation of any gambling game, cashless wagering system or drop box, or any electronic or mechanical device connected thereto, or for removing money or other contents therefrom.

*Applies to Nevada State Law, and may or may not be in compliance with other state laws and regulations.

5. It is unlawful for any person to have on his person or in his possession any paraphernalia for manufacturing slugs. As used in this subsection, "paraphernalia for manufacturing slugs" means the equipment, products and materials that are intended for use or designed for use in manufacturing, producing, fabricating, preparing, testing, analyzing, packaging, storing or concealing a counterfeit facsimile of the chips, tokens, debit instruments or other wagering instruments approved by the state gaming control board or a lawful coin of the United States, the use of which is unlawful pursuant to subsection 2. The term includes, but is not limited to:

    a. Lead or lead alloys;

    b. Molds, forms or similar equipment capable of producing a likeness of a gaming token or United States coin;

    c. Melting pots or other receptacles;

    d. Torches;

    e. Tongs, trimming tools or other similar equipment; and

    f. Equipment which can be reasonably demonstrated to manufacture facsimiles of debit instruments or wagering instruments approved by the state gaming control board.

6. Possession of more than one of the devices, equipment, products or materials described in this section permits a rebuttable inference that the possessor intended to use them for cheating.

149.

Fraudulent Acts*

It is unlawful for any person:

1. To alter or misrepresent the outcome of a game or other event on which wagers have been made after the outcome is made sure but before it is revealed to the players.

2. To place, increase or decrease a bet or to determine the course of play after acquiring knowledge, not available to all players, of the outcome of the game or any event that affects the outcome of the game or which is the subject of the bet or to aid anyone in acquiring such knowledge for the purpose of placing, increasing or decreasing a bet or determining the course of play contingent upon that event or outcome.

3. To claim, collect or take, or attempt to claim, collect or take, money or anything of value in or from a gambling game, with the intent to defraud, without having made a wager contingent thereon, or to claim, collect or take an amount greater than the amount won.

4. Knowingly to entice or induce another to go to any place where a ambling game is being conducted or operated in violation of the provisions of this chapter, with the intent that the other person play or participate in that gambling game.

5. To place or increase a bet after acquiring knowledge of the outcome of the game or other event which is the subject of the bet, including past-posting and pressing bets.

6. To reduce the amount wagered or cancel the bet after acquiring knowledge of the outcome of the game or other event which is the subject of the bet, including pinching bets.

7. To manipulate, with the intent to cheat, any component of a gaming device in a manner contrary to the designed and normal operational purpose for the component, including, but not limited to, varying the pull of the handle of a slot machine, with knowledge that the manipulation affects the outcome of the game or with knowledge of any event that affects the outcome of the game.

---

*Nevada State Law NRS465.070, 465.080. Applies to Nevada state law, and may or may not be in compliance with other state laws and regulations.

150.

Courtroom Demeanor

Once your team conducts an investigation resulting in an arrest, you must know how to take it through the court system. This is where your efforts are gone through with a fine-toothed comb.

Preparation

1. Read all investigative reports, especially the ones written by you.

2. Re-read your report.

3. Review all photos and tapes.

4. Examine all physical evidence, if available, without damaging its integrity or chain of custody.

5. Revisit the crime scene if possible, taking mental pictures and directional guidance.

6. Consult with the prosecutor.

7. Make visual aids, especially for a jury trial, if necessary.

8. Prepare technical data.

9. Do not omit any evidence unless otherwise instructed to do so by the court.

Role as a Witness

1. Remember that you are on display, including your morals and integrity.

2. Keep your purpose for being there on your mind.

3. There is no reason to act any other way than as your natural self.

4. Dress, act, and speak appropriately.

5. Let the prosecutor do his or her work; do not attempt to help unless specifically asked.

6. Do not attempt to try to fool or mislead the defense; it will only be obvious and damage your case.

7. Use common everyday language, especially during a jury trial. Professional jargon can be intimidating to a jury.

8. Always answer questions with a direct yes or no, unless otherwise instructed to expand by the court.

Things to Bring

1. Your copy of the subpoena with all data correctly and accurately completed.

2. Your original notes and your report, for the purpose of refreshing your memory while on the witness stand. Always request first that the court allow you to refresh your memory by using these means.

3. All evidence requested of you, making sure chain of custody is always adhered to.

4. Your Miranda card if used during the arrest, ready to present if asked.

5. Knowledge of your past training and experience if you are asked to be regarded as a professional witness.

The Steps of a Trial

1. Pre-trial motion and hearings.

2. Jury selection.

3. Opening statements to the jury.

4. Oath and exclusionary procedures of witness(s).

5. Direct examination by both the prosecutor and the defense.

6. Cross-examinations.

7. Objections. When they are made, stay completely quiet until the judge advises you to answer the question or not.

8. Final arguments to the jury.

9. Jury deliberations and verdict.

10. Sentencing.

11. Appeals.

Appearance

Look and act as the trained professional that you are. Show the court your respect through your dress as well as your demeanor.

Testifying in Court

1. Treat all court participants with courtesy.

2. Speak the full truth on all matters with which you have direct knowledge when asked.

3. Listen carefully to all questions asked of you.

4. Think out your answer prior to your response.

5. Speak clearly so all can hear with clarity.

6. Do not use gestures. You are speaking to a recorder.

7. Never guess an answer.

8. If you make an error in your response, correct it immediately.

9. If you do not understand the question completely, request that the question be repeated.

10. Never overanalyze or try to read between the lines of any question; answer directly.

11. Never exaggerate, just state the facts

12. Do not attempt to get creative. It will hurt your case.

13. Always look directly into the eyes of the one(s) asking the questions.

14. Do not ignore the presence of the jury. Make eye contact. Speak to them, not at them.

Glossary

Glossary

The casino industry uses a specialized terminology. We are going to list terms that have not been defined elsewhere, with a brief definition for each. These terms should be known to anyone employed within the gaming industry.

1. **Ace:** Usually the highest card in the deck; can also be counted as a one, as in blackjack, or for straights in poker games.

2. **Action button:** Usually a disk or rectangle made of plastic, sometimes with different colors or writing on each side to identify the type of action or where the betting action will begin. Used in a number of Asian games, exotic games, and poker, while playing hold'em.

3. **Advantage player:** Very skilled play based on knowledge of the game, the value of the cards, the cards that have been played, and the cards remaining in the deck. Includes card counting and shuffle tracking. Advantage play is not cheating.

4. **Agent:** 1.An employee of a local or state gaming authority, also known as a gaming agent. 2. An outside agent, referred to in law as a coconspirator or accomplice, who helps a dealer or other employee steal from the casino. Someone that is not an employee of the casino. It could even be an operator of a carnival game.

5. **Ante:** A fee collected from each player before the cards are dealt, primarily used in the game of poker. Also used in a few exotic games such as Caribbean stud and three card poker, where a fee is collected before a player can join the game or some type of progressive jackpot.

6. **Apron:** A piece of cloth designed to be worn by dealers, which fastens around the waist. It prevents wear and tear on the clothing of the dealer, and the gaming equipment, and also it makes it a little bit harder for them to get to their pockets.

7. **Back-to-back:** Two cards with the same denomination, consisting of the hole card and the card dealt up.

8. **Bank:** 1. The chip tray or the chips on a table game such as blackjack or craps. 2. The money in a cash drawer or cart for a cashier, change booth or change person.

9. **Bar:** Aside from a place to where you would go to enjoy a refreshing beverage, *bar* also means to exclude or prohibit a person from playing on your property or from even entering your property.

10. **Betting square:** The area, consisting of a circle, square, or logo on a casino table, where players are to place their wagers.

11. **Big six:** Also known as the *wheel of fortune*, an old-time casino game where the winning bet is decided by a large spinning wheel.

12. **Bill validator:** A device on a slot machine which accepts, reads, and either rejects currency or sends it to the *drop* can, adding credits to the machine for the patron to play.

13. **Black(s):** Another name for a one-hundred-dollar chip.

14. **Black book:** Originated and primarily used in Nevada. It is a compilation of people who are officially barred from casinos due to criminal activities or associations that would be a threat to the casino industry.

15. **Blind:** Sometimes called a big blind. Normally used in the game of poker it is the second position clockwise from the action button, which designates a forced minimum bet of a player.

16. **Bones:** A slang name for dice.

17. **Border work:** Markings added by cheaters to the printed borderlines of cards to identify their value.

18. **Bottoms:** To deal a card off the bottom of the deck rather than the top. A very skilled cheating technique; the cards do not necessarily have to come from the bottom of the deck, although they are still referred to as bottoms.

19. **Boxman:** The person on a crap game who is responsible for the table bank and who is also the first level supervisor for the three dealers on the game.

20. **Box person (or boxman):** This commonly refers to a member of the dice pit who sits on the game and is in charge of the integrity of the game as well as the chips in the game. Somewhat like a lifeguard watching over a busy pool.

21. **Break a hand:** On blackjack, to receive or be dealt cards with total values exceeding a total of twenty-one. Also known as *busting*.

22. **Break-in:** Known in most circles as a rookie. In the casino business, a break-in is a person with little or no dealing experience.

23. **Break it down:** To cut checks into countable piles, as dictated within internal controls.

24. **Break the deck:** On blackjack, to shuffle before the entire deck is played out.

25. **Bridge:** A gapping or bent card, used to signal the player where to cut the cards. Or telling the player what the next card is.

26. **Brief:** A very old term, primarily an individual card in the deck used to steer the person cutting the deck to the most suitable location.

27. **Bug:** A device fastened beneath the table by a cheater to hold out a card or cards. This is usually made of metal to hold the card with tension against the table or within the grasp of the cheater.

28. **Burn card:** The first card taken from the top of the deck after the shuffle and cut and placed on the discard tray or into the muck.

29. **Bury the hole card:** To place the dealer's second card under the first card so that it is completely covered.

30. **Buy-in:** The amount of cash the player initially starts with.

31. **C note:** A slang word for a one-hundred-dollar bill.

32. **Cage:** The "bank" in a casino where players change chips for cash and establish and record credit transactions. Source for fills, and the central location for all money transactions and records.

33. **Cap:** 1. When a twenty one dealer pays a winning bet by putting the payoff on top of the player's original bet rather than sizing into it or cutting into it to make even stacks. 2. To add to a bet after cards are received. (See also *press* and *pinch*.)

34. **Card counting:** Using a memory system to keep track of cards that have been dealt and what cards remain in the deck. The basic counting system is comprised of a plus-minus or high-low system.

35. **Card switching:** Card switching is done by one player playing two hands or by a team. These individuals are very fast with sleight-of-hand movements.

36. **Case bet:** The player's final bet from his available funds.

37. **Case card:** The last card in the deck to be given value.

38. **Cash-out:** 1. When a player exchanges lower-value chips for larger-value chips upon discontinuing play. Sometimes a cover-up will take place, and the cash-out will be given to the dealer and the dealer will supplement the cash-out with higher-denomination chips which more than equal the value. 2. Converting credits on a slot machine to coin, cash, or other form which can be changed to cash.

39. **Casino surveillance:** * The department which has the capability to observe and record activities being conducted in a licensed gaming establishment. This is done primarily with CCTV cameras and video recording. Many surveillance departments also use agents on the casino floor. They also have access to paper trails from internal audits, and many other resources.

40. **Catch:** 1. A common phrase used by gamblers when they receive a given card or hand they just had to have, or felt they needed to have, to win the game. 2. To see or receive information, not generally available to a player, such as the dealer's hole card.

41. **Center field:** A generic term for a person in the middle seat of the betting area or the layout of the gaming table.

42. **Chase:** Playing longer and stronger to win back funds that have been lost.

43. **Cheque(s):** Tokens used on table games with specific denominations, usually one dollar, five dollars, twenty-five dollars, one-hundred dollars, five-hundred dollars, one-thousand dollars, and up.

44. **Cheque carrier:** A plastic carrier used primarily by security personnel to transport cheques to and from the casino cage.

45. **Cheque play:** A general term called out by a dealer to get a supervisor's attention when a large bet or bets are placed.

46. **Cheque rack:** A tray on a gaming table, normally made of metal or wood, used to store and organize the chips used to play the game.

47. **Chip(s):** Tokens used on gaming tables. Can mean *cheque* or refer to nonvalued tokens on a roulette game.

*Applies to Nevada State Law, and may or may not be in compliance with other state laws and regulations.

48. **Chip cup:** A cheating device manufactured and painted to the finest precision standards to look like a stack of chips.

49. **Clean money:** Normally refers to the checks that come directly out of the rack to a player.

50. **Clearing your hands:** An internal control established in the vast majority of casinos. The dealer (and often anyone who handles money or chips) is required to actually clap and show their palms face up with the fingers spread, so all gaming personnel and especially surveillance can clearly see that before their leaving the game, they have no chips or articles of the game in their hands. A dealer would also clear his or her hands before going to any part of his or her body, such as a pocket.

51. **Color change:** Primarily converting lower denomination chips into higher denomination chips. In other words, giving five one-dollar chips for one five-dollar chip.

52. **Cooler decks:** A deck of cards that are presorted and arranged so that when the cards are dealt to a specific number of hands, all players' hands will be winners if played correctly.

53. **Cosmetics:** An old term that refers to daubs. They can be ashes, lip gloss or any type of substance that would mark a card for a player to use. Luminous inks, dyes, waxes, and crayons can be used by cheaters to mark cards—anything that will get the job done.

54. **Credit:** A term used in the casino just like any other business. It is money a casino fronts to a player with the agreement that it will be paid back. All credit transactions have a documentation process that must be followed, and a lot of internal policies and procedures. Large amounts of credit can involve state or federal types of paperwork.

55. **Credit slip:** Paperwork that accompanies a credit at the table game when chips are removed from the table and returned to the cage.

56. **Croupier:** A dealer on baccarat who handles the cards. On craps, the stickman, who handles the dice. A roulette dealer.

57. **Daub:** Colored paste or other materials used by card cheats to mark cards during play. (See also *cosmetics*.)

58. **Dedicated camera:*** A video camera required to continuously record a specific activity. In lieu of continuous recording, time-lapse recording is acceptable if approved, in advance, by the gaming control board chairman or his or her designee. Dedicated cameras are normally fixed in position to record a specific area, table, or machine.

59. **Dice bowl:** Normally made of wood or rubber, it stores the dice that are not being used by the players. A normal number of dice to be put on a game would be five, so three would stay in the bowl, and of course two would be used at a time.

60. **Dirty stack:** A stack of chips of different denominations, intermingled and not broken down correctly by a dealer.

61. **Discard tray (or rack):** The plastic object, usually red, attached to the table to receive cards that have already been played. This device holds the cards until the next shuffle. History has it that discard trays were purposely made with a special red material that was able to reveal certain markings used on cards so they could be inspected in the discard tray by supervisors.

62. **Double deal:** Dealing two cards together instead of one.

63. **Double down:** On blackjack, to bet twice the amount of the original bet and then receive only one hit card.

64. **Down cards:** Cards that are dealt face down.

65. **Drop:** 1. The total amount of cash, markers, or other forms of exchange in the table game the drop boxes. 2. The gross amount of money received by the casino, or a part of the casino, such as slots or pit, in a specific period—a shift, day, month, quarter, etc.

66. **Drop box:** Where the money is put when the players buy in to the casino games. The moneys go in the box and the chips go to the player. The drop box holds many records such as markers, fills, and credits. Also known as *can.*

67. **Drop cut:** A skilled technique used to pay bets. The dealer drops a specific number of chips to pay a bet from a stack of chips in his hand. This is a technique used mostly on craps and roulette. (See also *sizing in.*)

---

*Applies to Nevada State Law, and may or may not be in compliance with other state laws and regulations.

68. **Dump:** Overpaying players on a bet. *Dumping a game* refers to emptying the tray and indicates that managers feel that something crooked is happening.

69. **Edge:** The advantage in favor of the house or the player.

70. **Exposed card:** A card that is accidentally shown during the play that would not normally be shown.

71. **Eye in the sky:** Has always meant surveillance.

72. **Face card:** A king, queen, or jack

73. **False cut:** A move that appears to cut the deck but does not.

74. **False deal:** Any deal in which other than the proper cards are dealt.

75. **False shuffle:** Any technique that would make it appear that a deck is being shuffled when it is not.

76. **Fill:** 1. Chips brought to a game to replenish the table bank. 2. An amount of coin put into a slot machine hopper when it is emptied by jackpots and smaller payoffs.

77. **Fill Slip:** The document that accompanies the chips in a fill, which gives an exact amount in each denomination, and an exact total, for the chips being brought to the table.

78. **First Base:** The first player position on a twenty-one table. The player who receives the first card.

79. **Flash:** When the dealer exposes the top card on the deck which is the next card to be dealt. Either intentional or unintentional. If intentional it is intended to help the player win. Also refers to exposing the dealer's hole card.

80. **Flat store:** Casinos in the old days, when they cheated customers. Also known as a *crooked carnival game*.

81. **Floor man or floor person:** Supervisor of gaming tables.

82. **Flop:** In poker, the community cards exposed while playing hold 'em or different types of hold 'em such as pineapple, Omaha, etc.

83. **Foreign chips:** Chips from other casinos. This does not mean from another country.

84. **Front money:** A sum of money that a player deposits into the cashiers cage which he borrows (signs *markers* against) while in play. It is a good way for someone to keep his or her money in safekeeping. (See also *marker*.)

85. **George:** A player or patron who tips very well.

86. **Going south:** Slang terminology for a player placing checks in his or her pocket during the course of play on a casino game. Also refers to employee theft.

87. **Green:** 1. A dealer who is inexperienced. 2. The name given to a twenty-five-dollar denomination cheque.

88. **Grind joint:** A casino where most of its action is of low limits.

89. **Heads up:** A player playing alone against the dealer.

90. **Hole card:** The face-down card of the dealer.

91. **House:** The casino.

92. **House dealer:** A dealer who genuinely wants to win for the house.

93. **Hustle:** When a dealer or other casino personnel verbally encourages a player to toke the dealer or dealers.

94. **Hustler:** A gambling cheat or con artist.

95. **Imprest bank:** A specific amount of money in a cashier's change booths, or change person's cash bank, which must be exactly the same at the beginning and end of his or her shift.

96. **Insurance:** A side bet when the dealer shows an ace. This is when the player bets on whether or not the dealer has a twenty-one. It pays two to one, and may only be made to half the amount of the original bet.

97. **Juice:** 1. Another name for a commission or vig that a player must pay, for example, in a baccarat game. 2. A connection or someone that you know who may be an influential person, or that person's influence.

98. **Lammer:** Used by dealer, floor person, and supervisor, as well as surveillance, a small disk with numerical value that is put on the table to indicate

cate marker play, money, or credit owed to that table by the cashier's cage or to show that money was removed from that table. It designates the amount of money moved. Lammers are also used to track the total buy-in on crap games and to mark the value of chips on roulette games.

99. **Limit:** The maximum bet per hand allowed on a table.

100. **Live card:** A card that has not been dealt or put into play.

101. **Locator:** A card in a deck that has been marked to indicate the value or the beginning of a particular clump of cards.

102. **Mark:** A victim or intended target of any con game or of a pickpocket or distract-and-grab team.

103. **Marker:** A credit instrument. Should a player have money deposited in the cage or credit established in the cage, a player may ask for a marker, which is now a credit instrument, and it will be held against the funds he or she has on credit or deposit. The player will then cash in the markers or pay the markers at the end of his or her play.

104. **Marker play:** To play using funds recorded as cash on deposit or credit at the cage.

105. **Mechanic:** A person who has perfected the skill and art of sleight of hand while handling cards.

106. **Misdeal:** A faulty deal resulting in a redeal.

107. **Money plays:** A call made out by the dealer to the supervisor when currency is used for the bet or the wager.

108. **Motion activated dedicated camera:*** A video camera and VCR that, upon detection of activity or motion in a specific area, begins to record the activity or area.

109. **Mucker/mucking:** A player with cards hidden on his or her person who puts the cards into play at the right time.

110. **Nail:** To catch individuals cheating or stealing.

111. **Nailing:** A cheating technique used to mark cards by simply putting a dent in the card with a fingernail, or a device such as a pin or a chip.

---

*Applies to Nevada State Law, and may or may not be in compliance with other state laws and regulations.

112. **Nickels:** Slang for five-dollar chips.

113. **Nonvalue chip(s):** On roulette, chips that have no specific value until assigned by the dealer according to their color when the player buys in. Normally valued at the table minimum but can be assigned a higher value.

114. **On the river:** A common poker term that refers to the last card dealt in that poker hand.

115. **Paddle:** The device used to push the currency and paperwork into the metal drop box. When used, it pushes the money in and seals the hole at the top of the table so nothing can get in unless the paddle is removed.

116. **Paint:** Face cards such as a jack, queen, or king are commonly referred to as paints.

117. **Painter:** This is a card cheat who specializes in daubing the cards during a play.

118. **Pair splitting:** On blackjack, when a player is dealt a pair on his or her original hand, he or she may split them into two separate hands. He must match his original bet for the second hand.

119. **Pick up a marker:** The marker has been paid off.

120. **Pip:** The spots on the cards that indicate the suit as well as the denomination of the card.

121. **Pit:** 1. A group of table games in a specified area. 2. The personnel and department of the casino concerned with table games.

122. **Pit boss:** The supervisor of the pit. Can refer to any supervisor in the pit, either floor supervisor or, higher, pit manager.

123. **Pocket:** The term for hole cards, usually used in poker.

124. **Pot:** The amount wagered in a given hand. Again normally used in poker.

125. **Power of the pen:** A term that refers to someone who has the authority to write out a comp without having to go to a higher authority.

126. **Progression:** A system in betting in which the player increases the bet after every win. A *losing progression* increases the wager after each loss.

127. **PTZ camera:*** A video camera that possesses, at a minimum, pan, tilt and zoom capabilities or features comparable thereto.

128. **Push or tie:** The dealer and player have the same value hands. No one wins, no one loses.

129. **Pushing off:** The dealer is giving chips to an outside agent or coconspirator that they have not rightfully won.

130. **Rack:** 1. The chip tray on a table game, also called the tray or bank. 2. A plastic tray that holds slot tokens.

131. **Rake:** The fee collected from the pot. Again, normally used in poker; it is determined by the house, state laws, regulations, etc.

132. **Rating:** Evaluation of a patron's play for the purpose of finding out how much he "deserves" in terms of complimentary services. Ratings give an evaluation based on the amount of wagers places over an amount of time.

133. **Reds:** A term for five-dollar cheques.

134. **Relief dealer:** The individuals who are assigned to give breaks, or the dealer who comes to relieve you at the end of your shift.

135. **Riffle/riffle stack:** This is the part of the shuffle when the cards are put together and interlaced.

136. **Rim play:** Credit play that does not require a signed marker. See also *marker*.

137. **Round robin:** This is the system by which dealers take breaks. If you have four dealers, each would work table number one, table number two, table three, and dealer number four is on a break.

138. **Rubber band:** Another dealer break system. Out of sixteen dealers in one pit, twelve are dealing and four are on break at any time. When four return from break, the pit bosses moves a rubber band down a list to tell him which dealers are next to be relieved. This system is used most often when the number of dealers does not allow an even division of breaks.

139. **Run it down:** 1. To cut down the cheques to verify the amount; in the table bank, you run the bank down or the tray down. 2. To run down the

---

*Applies to Nevada State Law, and may or may not be in compliance with other state laws and regulations.

shoe or the deck: when a surveillance department is reviewing the tape to determine if someone may in fact be an advantage player.

140. **Satellite surveillance equipment:*** Surveillance monitors, recorders, remote selectors and other ancillary equipment located in an area other than the surveillance room and used for casino surveillance.

141. **Shill:** A player who is employed by the casino to play with house funds to help get a game started or keep one going. Often used in poker but rarely used in twenty-one.

142. **Shoe:** A device that holds several decks of cards, used in dealing multiple-deck blackjack and other games such as baccarat.

143. **Silver:** Commonly, one-dollar tokens or any type of change that is used on a gambling game.

144. **Silver miner(s):** People who make a living walking through casinos collecting abandoned credits and coins on slot machines.

145. **Sizing in:** A technique for playing even-money bets on most table games. The dealer does not need to know or calculate the amount of the bet. He or she simply cuts a stack of chips of the same denomination with his or her index finger so that the bet and payoff are the same amount.

146. **Slot change booth:*** A structure on the floor of a licensed gaming establishment that houses a coin-counting device used to redeem coins from patrons. The term does not include slot-machine change carousels, floor banks, or change banks.

147. **Slug:** 1. The cards not dealt at the end of the shoe. Also, a group of cards that are not interlaced during a shuffle or a group of cards that may be interlaced, but both stacks were of high or low denomination, creating a slug. 2. A false token or coin made of lead, played into a slot machine to cheat the machine in place of currency or a real token or change.

148. **Snapper:** A natural twenty-one, or blackjack. A picture card and an ace received as the first two cards.

149. **Soft hand:** A hand that contains one or two aces on the first two cards but not a ten or a face card.

*Applies to Nevada State Law, and may or may not be in compliance with other state laws and regulations.

150. **Sorts:** Cards that arrive from the factory that are not cut evenly. A method of cheating that distinguishes certain cards by size or differences in the way the pattern on the back of the card has been cut.

151. **Split:** Commonly, in blackjack, when two cards of equal value are turned into two separate hands. The original bet must be matched to split a hand.

152. **Spread the cards:** To spread the cards on the layout wide enough so that the players, the dealers, the shift managers, and surveillance can see what every card is.

153. **Square up the deck:** To straighten out the deck so that all cards are neatly aligned.

154. **Stiff:** 1. A blackjack hand less than seventeen, such as a fourteen or a fifteen. 2. A player who does not toke.

155. **Strip:** 1. An action made during a shuffle that rearranges the order of the cards: to strip the deck. 2. Slang for Las Vegas Boulevard in Las Vegas, Nevada, or the Sunset Strip in Los Angeles.

156. **Sub:** A device or pocket used to transport a chip that h A secure location(s) in a licensed gaming establishment used primarily for casino surveillance.

158. **Surveillance system:*** A system of video cameras, monitors, recorders, video printers, switches, selectors, and other ancillary equipment used for casino surveillance.

159. **Sweat:** When a casino employee or management openly displays concerns about certain individual or individuals that may be winning a lot of money.

160. **Table assignment:** Another system for dealer breaks. Each dealer is assigned to stay at a particular table except for the time when he or she is on break. Usually, you would need assigned relief dealers to break each table.

161. **Table game(s):** Games run by a casino in which the casino is betting against the player, such as blackjack, craps, roulette, and baccarat. Does not include games such as poker, where the house makes its money by a per-hand or per-time fee.

---

*Applies to Nevada State Law, and may or may not be in compliance with other state laws and regulations.

162. **Take a shot:** An attempt to cheat a game or to gain more payout from a game by lying about a particular bet placement, etc.

163. **Toke:** A tip or gratuity.

164. **Toke committee:** Dealers who are appointed by their peers that are in charge of collecting and dispersing and documenting tokes in an even distribution to all the other dealers.

165. **Tray:** The rack on a gaming table that houses the money or chips.

166. **Turning (or rolling) the deck:** When a shuffle has been completed the dealer will shout this out. The deck is being turned to its side for the player to use the cut card.

167. **Up card:** This is the dealer's top card or the card that is showing.

168. **Walk the table:** The dealer changes position behind the table by moving sideways. This enables the dealer to always keep the table tray in sight, as well as all of the cards and players, never turning his or her back to any position at the table.

169. **Weight:** Loaded dice

170. **Whale:** An individual who is a very high limit player.

Appendices

Appendix I

From the U.S. Department of Justice Office of Justice Programs, National Institute of Justice. Research Review. Vol. 2 Issue 3. November 2001

Effects of Casino Gambling on Crime and Quality of Life in New Casino Jurisdictions, Final Report, G. Stitt.

This study found that when casinos are introduced in a community, the impact on crime varies by community. No single "casino effect" was found. Researchers analyzed crime data for 4 years before and after casinos opened in seven communities in Illinois, Iowa, Missouri, and Mississippi. Data were collected on (1) crimes committed, (2) community perceptions, and (3) quality-of-life issues, such as gambling addiction, suicide and bankruptcy. In three cities-Sioux City, Biloxi, and Peoria –many more crimes significantly increased than decreased. In three other communities – St. Louis, St. Louis Country, and Alton –many more crimes significantly decreased than increased. Residents generally believed the casinos increased crime, whereas community leaders generally believed casinos increased the quality of life and helped the economy. The research suggests that community leaders who are considering approving the presence of casinos should seek advice on preparation methods from well established casino communities. 194 pp. Grant 98-IJ-CX-0037;NCJ 187679. The full abstract can be found at: http://www.ncjrs.org/rr/vol2_3/14.html. See also "Casino Gambling: Burdon or Boon? NIJ Journal, April 2001 (JR000247) at: http://www.ojp.usdoj.gov/nij/journals.

Appendix II

Fifty Things You Need To Know About Being A Successful Supervisor/Manager:

Listed below are brief capsules of what it would take for you to expand your role and become an effective supervisor and, with continued self-improvement and development, a manager.

1. **Understanding people.** You must understand the behavior of the people you supervise. Learn who your people are, their needs, and their desire to be treated fairly and with dignity.

2. **Coaching.** Learn what it takes to get your people moving in the right direction to achieve the desired results.

3. **Communication.** Learn the cultural requirements to communicate effectively within your specific organization. What does it require to get the necessary information or requests to flow up and down the organizational chain?

4. **Leadership when there is no one else around.** In the absence of a higher authority, you may be required to exercise judgment or authority that may exceed your charter. Be prepared to exercise common sense and to logically address the situation.

5. **Developing the star.** It is often said that a good leader develops his or her own replacement. Do not be afraid to develop those beneath you, as they will attest to your success.

6. **Internal memos and communication.** Learn to use the methods of internal communications in the organization as a teaching or instructing tool for those beneath you in the chain of command.

7. **Reality shock.** An event of major proportions that causes you to realign your thinking , i.e., stock market crash.

8. **Power and influence.** Every supervisor and manager has a level of power. Exercise power with discretion and never abuse it. Influence is entirely different from power but frequently goes hand in hand with power. Not all with power can effectively influence others. This is particularly true when attempting to influence those higher in the organizational chain.

9. **Dealing with high-performance employees.** This type of employee, while valuable and desirable, is often difficult to manage. The care, attention,

praise, and other tools necessary to sustain performance requires your effort. You may be asked to provide a variety of skills to maintain the employee's continued peak performance.

10. **Dealing with hard lessons as a first-time supervisor or manager.** Learn to accept that not all those above you in the chain of command are consistent or even skilled in the position they hold. This may be revealed by such events as the first time you are not supported in a decision you have made.

11. **Becoming a supervisor or manager.** Through diligence and hard work you can create the responses necessary to those in a position to advance your career. It is advisable to understand the model to follow that has been achieved by others to reach this goal.

12. **Assisting and supporting new supervisors or managers.** Adopting a cooperative team player attitude in your peer and superior relationships is a positive and logical pursuit to compliment your own performance. It is the right thing to do.

13. **Retaining midcareer management.** Organizations should do all they can do to prevent the loss of trained and experienced midlevel managers who are successful and effective in their role. It is cost effective and preserves continuity.

14. **Reflections on retention of managers.** The saying "If it ain't broke, don't allow it to break down" immediately comes to mind. If you are managing fairly and compensating appropriately, then the causes for management discontent leading to leaving the organization are minimized. It is obvious that there may be other motivations for making change. It would be wise to review all the conditions to determine what may have affected the decision to leave.

15. **Micromanagers.** The quickest method to frustrate employees is to micromanage them. This does not allow the employee to feel creative, participatory, and involved, and the sense of self-worth and productivity diminish.

16. **Managers managing.** The ultimate responsibility of a manager is to guide individuals within the organization to the corporate goal and mission.

17. **Profiles of supervisors and managers.** Organizations have particular profiles and images that they have developed or created. The successful candidate should have this, look like that, or have the following education, to name but a few. Frequently such a profile is assumed or simply is

the "way it's always been." Depending on the organization and the type of business it conducts, this can be either a good or a bad situation.

18. **Analyzing your influence style.** Just what kind of manager or supervisor are you? How do you influence others whom you supervise to get the task at hand completed on time and without mistakes? There are various methods to influence or manage others. What style is needed depends on what type of constituency you are trying to manage.

19. **The operational unit.** Throughout all of work history it is the doers who lay claim to being the most important unit in the workplace. Nobody else would have a job if it were not for them! Managers must teach the importance of the operational unit as a part of the team.

20. **Corporate philosophy.** The values by which the organization operates, the fundamental beliefs by which the organization elects to be known and its guidelines for doing business.

21. **Working women.** Without them, what would any organization be? The force and impact of the working woman since World War II has successfully changed and improved the workplaces of the world.

22. **Exercising authority.** Authority over a worker is a bridge between the goal of an idea and the desired result. How the manager uses his or her authority has a tremendous influence upon the workforce.

23. **Setting the stage as a manager.** The arena in which the span of influence that the specific manager has to manage might well be a stage. How he or she directs and orchestrates the resources that he or she manages to accomplish tasks must, at the least, be well thought out, fair, and logically implemented.

24. **Coping with stress**. It is a given that managers are frequently stressed. Even in the best of organizations, stress is a factor. It should never be ignored or neglected. Stress in the workplace is not limited to managers, and good managers learn to recognize its presence within the workforce. Since stress can be triggered by the process of work or by outside influences, it is important that the manager know of the organizational resources available to address the condition. The manager must avoid becoming the cause of stress.

25. **The corporate manager.** Frequently misunderstood and maligned as being an inhabitant of a mythical Ivory Tower, the corporate manager is a critical member of the team. It must be remembered that they are the ultimate communicators of information up and down the chain. They are an instrument of the organization to accomplish corporate goals.

26. **Making the system work.** The manager is a conductor who orchestrates all the resources to accomplish assigned tasks. When problems arise or obstructions develop, he or she must find ways to negotiate or overcome the specific condition regardless of what the cause is.

27. **Methodology to implement change.** Given the parameters in which to implement change for which the manager is accountable, he or she must analyze the situation and develop a plan. The plan is dependent upon the conditions that are present, the resources available to affect change, the preparation of the workers to understand and adjust. Under all circumstances and conditions you still have basic ingredients that must be present. Trust, communication, and loyalty are but a few.

28. **Myths of a "perfect" manager or mentors.** They are never wrong or make mistakes. They know more than you do about how to get the job accomplished.

29. **Having a one-on-one work relationship.** The optimum word is *work*. A successful supervisor or manager needs to have sources of feedback in the workplace. The measure of effectiveness of your efforts includes the following: Are you understood? Are you being fair? Do you really know what the work conditions are? Do your changes have or receive the proper support, equipment, raw material, information?

30. **Creative managers.** They have a method for getting things accomplished or completed in spite of negative conditions or situations. They have a way of making work easy and fun.

31. **Action plans.** They key word is *action*. Sometimes an action plan does not achieve its purpose. That is part of what a good manager does; he or she can smooth the path to accomplishing the task at hand when action plans fall short. We know that to accomplish anything and to have a start and a finish, we must have a plan of action. They are not always correct or without flaws. Remember Murphy's Law.

32. **Leadership and organizational behaviors.** Companies and their leaders seem to get what they deserve. Reputations, both good and bad, are achieved by the types of examples that the leadership or owners establish. Ethics, fairness, quality, honesty are the foundation of a positive business reputation. It is the culture of the organization.

33. **The right or wrong influence.** This directly effects enthusiasm toward work. Keeping an open mind about changes or suggestions about improving the work process by a manager will not send negative influences.

34. **Managing with new office technology.** The manager or supervisor who resists new technology or refuses to accept process changes, particularly with operational administrative controls or procedures, is doomed to be less effective and accepted. Methods to track time and attendance, productivity, quality performance, and considerable other information about operational and administrative concerns have resulted in numerous changes in the workplace.

35. **Organizational priorities.** The management and supervision, be it good or bad or somewhere in between, is the instrument of carrying out the organizational priorities. It asserts the priorities and implements the plan(s) to achieve them.

36. **Budgets or financial goals.** Costs are a factor of life for any manager. Organizations, be they for profit or services, are all guided by financial considerations. The manager must follow formations of budgets just like any other plan. They must be realistic and in conformity with the requests of the organizational plan. They must be fair and reasonable and realistically attainable.

37. **Research and development.** It is widely accepted that an organization is only as successful as its commitment to continue to seek improvement and change within its given field. The managers at all levels have an obligation to support any efforts by such groups within the organizations they manage. Communicating ideas, observations and feedback is part of that support. Complying with requests for cooperation and assistance is also a part of that support.

38. **Career opportunities.** Managers should not reject opportunities to accept greater challenge as a manager providing they have confidently demonstrated the attributes that provide the foundation for advancement. Preparing yourself is a very important part of being an effective manager. Availing yourself of the external and internal personal development opportunities should be a part of your plan.

39. **Risks.** Learn to take calculated risks that can improve conditions both for the tasks at hand and for your own development. Do not be faint of heart.

40. **Fundamentals of motivation.** Everybody responds positively to recognition and praise. But frequently, managers do not include such ingredients as listening, understanding, being nonjudgmental, providing the necessary items to achieve, resolving conflicts, and providing a neat and happy environment.

41. **Bad attitudes.** Employees and managers at times both have bad attitudes toward each other, as well as toward the corporate goals. Individuals with bad attitudes stand out, clearly.

42. **Decision making and problem solving.** The ability to analyze problems and determine the steps necessary to solve the problems.

43. **Delegating.** Giving employees authority to do the task, using proven methods.

44. **Hiring and firing.** Hiring, according to best practices, is not as stressful as firing an individual. It is still a management function that should not be overlooked.

45. **Time management.** Priority of one's time and one's responding to complete projects.

46. **Motivation.** This is the number-one priority of every supervisor—to motivate employees in a positive fashion.

47. **Discipline.** Every employee needs some form of positive evaluation in reference to job performance. Documentation is a key factor here.

48. **Goal setting.** There are two types of goals, short term and long term. Be careful not to set too many goals.

49. **The out-of-touch manager**. A manager who is not on the same track as the corporation and the rest of the department.

50. **Timing.** As managers, there are times when we should and should not step up to the plate. Know the climate. Know when to step forward or be prepared to be rejected.

Appendix III

Surveillance Lead Investigators Exam

Each question worth 5 points, 100 points a perfect score. Circle each answer.

1.   Nevada Revised Statue (NRS) 465.070 addresses which gaming crime?

   a. The unlawful dissemination of information concerning horse racing.
   b. Disposition of evidence.
   c. To alter or misrepresent the outcome of a game or other event on which wagers have been made after the outcome is made sure but before it is revealed to the player.

2.   A $27.00 blackjack pays

   a. $37.00
   b. $27.50
   c. $40.50

3.   If an advantage player is playing perfect **basic strategy**, and the **true count** has been determined, which of the following would dictate the player to **surrender** in a **multiple-deck** game?

   a. Players 20 vs. dealers ace up
   b. Players 14 vs. dealers ace up @a +3 game or greater
   c. Players 16 vs. dealers 5 up

4.   In order to shuffle track decks in the game of blackjack, deep shoe penetration is essential.

   a. True
   b. False

5.   An advantage player in the game of blackjack must use a betting spread to be effective.

   a. True
   b. False

6.   Gaming Control Board regulation 23 deals with:

   a. Slots
   b. Gaming tokens
   c. Poker

7. In mini-baccarat, if the player's first two cards total seven or more, the banker **must** stand and cannot draw a card.

    a. True
    b. False

8. In mini-baccarat, if the player's first two cards total six or more, the player **must** stand and may not draw a card.

    a. True
    b. False

9. In roulette, a split bet pays 16 to 1.

    a. True
    b. False

10. In roulette, a four number wager pays 8 to 1.

    a. True
    b. False

11. In slot terms, "return percentage" refers to what?

    a. The number of coins played kept by the casino
    b. The amount a slot machine returns on an average for every dollar played
    c. Casino advantage

12. State Gaming Regulation 5.010 deals with:

    a. Methods of operation
    b. Publication of payoffs
    c. Unauthorized games

13. When a casino player, after seeing his or her cards, increases the amount wagered, this action is called:

    a. Pressing
    b. Pinching
    c. Doubling down
    d. Counting

14. In roulette, a "street" bet pays:

    a. 3 to 1
    b. 5 to 1
    c. 11 to 1

15. In craps, the "come out" roll is always the first roll in an attempt to establish a point.

    a. True
    b. False

16. A 6A licensee shall not exchange cash for cash with or on behalf of a patron in any transaction in which the amount of the exchange is more than:

    a. $3,000.00
    b. $7,500.00
    c. $10,000.00

17. While counting down a six deck shoe in blackjack, and the running count is 8, and there are a total of two decks left to be dealt in the shoe, the true count conversion equals:

    a. −6
    b. +4
    c. +3

18. With today's technology, slot machines cannot be cheated.

    a. True
    b. False

19. In the game of Let It Ride, after the players review their hands, but **before** the dealer views a card, the player has an option of removing one of the three wagers.

    a. True
    b. False

20. The use of a sub by a dealer is:

    a. Any place on a dealer's person to conceal chips that have been stolen.
    b. When a dealer deals any card other than the top card.
    c. A card or dice mucking technique.

Surveillance Lead Investigators' Exam Answers

1) C

2) C

3) B

4) B

5) A

6) C

7) A

8) A

9) B

10) A

11) B

12) A

13) A

14) C

15) A

16) C

17) B

18) B

19) A

20) A

Index

Index

About the Authors

About the Authors

Gary L. Powell has over 17 years of investigative and casino gaming experience. His extensive career includes nine years with the Nevada State Gaming Control Board Enforcement Division. He is a gaming consultant for numerous Native American gaming properties to include conducting game protection seminars and surveillance room design. Mr. Powell was elected president of the worldwide Surveillance Information Network in 2001. He is a designer of satellite and DSL surveillance systems, and is highly trained in investigative, security, and game protection, and is proficient in establishing policies and directives for single and multiple hotel and casino surveillance and security operations.

Louis A. Tyska, CPP, is a private consultant, expert witness, and former chairman of the National Cargo Security Council. He has written, taught, and lectured widely in the security and business community. Together with Mr. Fennelly, he has co-authored several books, including *Security in the Year 2000 and Beyond*, *Cargo Theft Prevention: A Handbook for Logistics Security*, and *Retail Security: 150 Things You Should Know* and five others in that series. You may contact him at ltyska@aol.com

Lawrence J. Fennelly, CPO, CSS, is president of Litigation Consultants, Inc. He is a security consultant as well as a forensic consultant. He is the editor and author of numerous books on security issues. Among these many books is the widely read *Handbook of Loss Prevention and Crime Prevention*. This work is currently in its third edition, and is highly regarded in both public and private enforcement. You are invited to visit his website at www.litigationconsultants.com.